RUSSIA:
A MODERN HISTORY

David Warnes

Head of History, Ipswich School

Published by
Bell & Hyman
An imprint of Unwin Hyman Limited
Denmark House
37–39 Queen Elizabeth Street
London SE1 2QB

First published in 1984 by
University Tutorial Press Ltd

Reprinted 1987

ISBN 0 7135 2758 7

Printed in Great Britain by
Scotprint Ltd., Musselburgh

Acknowledgements

For permission to reproduce photographs we are grateful to the following:

Paul Popper Ltd. pages 4, 13, 22, 29 (*right*), 32, 33, 27 (*above*), 37, 43, 44, 53, 55, 56, 64, 65, 66, 75 (*below*), 78, 90, 99, 110, 115, 121, 123 (*left*), 127, 136, 139, 141, 148, 149, 151, 172, 174; Society for Cultural Relations with the U.S.S.R. pages 6, 16, 42 (*below*), 63, 84 (*and cover*), 98, 100, 102, 104, 123 (*right*), 128, 150, 171; Keystone Press Agency Ltd. pages 89, 118, 124, 138, 144, 152, 155, 158, 164, 168; The Mansell Collection Ltd. pages 2, 7, 21 (*right*), 28, 29 (*above*), 42 (*above*), 108; BBC Hulton Picture Library pages 21 (*left*), 27 (*below*), 57; Mary Evans Picture Library pages 26, 45, 48; Novosti Press Agency pages 15, 72, 74, 75 (*above*), 77, 120, 146, 169, 170, 173.

The author and publisher wish to thank all those who gave permission to reproduce material, the sources of which appear with the extracts. Also, the cartoon on page 91 is reproduced by permission of *The Standard*, the extract on page 3 by permission of Random House Inc, and the extract on page 60 (*Commissar: The Life and Death of Lavrenti Pavlovitch Beria* by Thaddeus Wittlin, Copyright © 1972 by Thaddeus Wittlin) by permission of Angus and Robertson Ltd. We would also like to thank Simon Boyd for drawing to our attention the contents of his grandmother Sybil Grey's diary (pages 38–9), and we thank Mary Sybil Boyd for permission to reproduce this material.

We have been unable to trace the copyright holders of a table of the Russian population (which appears on page 5) adapted from *The Decline of Imperial Russia* by Professor R. W. Seton-Watson, and *Russia* by Sir Donald Mackenzie Wallace, and would appreciate any information that would enable us to do so. Also we would be happy to hear from Progress Publishers in Moscow or their agents concerning permission for the extract on page 18. We acknowledge the estate of the late Sonia Brownell Orwell (page 67) and Penguin Books Ltd. (various).

Contents

Introduction

History is written from a point of view. Even the writer who sets out to be completely impartial is writing from a point of view – his view being that historians can and should try to be impartial.

This book contains documents and eyewitness accounts. Readers are invited to study them, to detect the point of view or bias of the writers and to compare different accounts of the same events and situations. These are some of the skills that professional historians use, though they are faced with a vast mass of evidence and the compass of this book only allows a small sample to be included.

The book also contains extracts from history books written and published in the U.S.S.R. The readers are invited to study these for evidence of their authors' point of view. They should also study the text of this book and look for clues to the present author's attitudes, remembering that what is *not* said in a history book is at least as important as what is said.

History is not cut and dried, and historians cannot simply say 'this is what happened and why'. They spend their time arguing with each other, and would want to argue over every sentence in this book.

Recent Russian history is plagued by the problem of the calendar. Until the Revolution the Russians clung to the Julian calendar, which had been abandoned in the West. Russia adopted the western calendar in 1918, by which time the Russians were thirteen days behind the rest of the world, so that by decree of the new Bolshevik government February 1st 1918 became February 14th 1918. I have used western dates, which is why the episodes known to historians as the February and October Revolutions appear to happen in March and November.

Historians writing about recent Russian history face the problem of how to refer to the country and its inhabitants. Strict accuracy demands that the former is referred to, after 1924, as 'the U.S.S.R.'. By the same token the latter are properly 'Soviet citizens'. I have, in the interests of variety, followed the practice of many other textbook writers and treated the terms 'Russia' and 'the U.S.S.R.' as interchangeable. I have also sometimes used the term 'the Russians' when referring to the population or the government of the U.S.S.R. When drawing a distinction between the Russian and non-Russian inhabitants of the Empire and the U.S.S.R. I have referred to the former as 'Great Russians'. These practices may not please purists, but they reflect current usage.

Russians use the Cyrillic alphabet, and Russian words have to be transliterated – changed from the Cyrillic to the Roman alphabet. In doing this I have tried to stick to familiar spellings. Chinese names are reproduced in the traditional Wade-Giles transliteration but in some cases I have added the modern or Pinyin version in brackets.

I would like to acknowledge the help and encouragement of a number of people: first and foremost my late father and my mother; Norman Stone, whose teaching first interested me in Russian history; and Andrew Milne and Alan Midgley, with whom I have had many stimulating discussions on this and other subjects. None of them, of course, bears any responsibility for the opinions expressed in the book.

1 Russia in 1900

The new Tsar

In 1894 Alexander III, Tsar (Emperor) of Russia, died. His son and heir, Nicholas II, married a German princess, Alix of Hesse-Darmstadt, three weeks after he ascended the throne. Alix, who was known to her Russian subjects as Alexandra, soon became the dominant influence in the life of her weak-willed husband. Nicholas' father had not prepared him for the tasks of government. Nicholas had been an officer in the army for a short time but was otherwise inexperienced. He and Alexandra believed that God had chosen his family, the Romanovs, to rule Russia and that it

was the duty of the people to obey their Tsar without question.

In theory Nicholas was an autocrat. There was no parliament to advise him or to limit his power. In practice the job of running the Empire was too complex for one man and the Tsar was forced to rely on ministers and civil servants. Their old-fashioned and inefficient administrative methods made it difficult to change or to improve the way in which Russia was governed. Nicholas knew that fear was an important part of his power. Though he saw himself as the 'father of his people', he intended to be a firm disciplinarian. His grandfather, Tsar Alexander II, had been killed by terrorists in 1881. The Tsar's Secret Police, the Okhrana, was not large enough and was only partially successful in rooting out terrorists and other opponents of the government.

Nicholas' and Alexandra's lifestyle was quite different from that of the majority of their subjects. They had an income equivalent to £12 000 000 a year in the values of those days, a retinue of 15 000 servants and numerous palaces and lesser residences stuffed with fine furniture and treasures. The great majority of their subjects were peasants.

1.1 Nicholas II and his wife Alexandra dressed in traditional royal robes, on the occasion of a fancy dress ball at the Winter Palace in St. Petersburg in 1903.

Landlords and Peasants

A peasant is a person who owns a plot of land and produces enough to feed his family but has little or nothing left to send to market. In 1900 roughly 75% of the land in Russia was worked by peasants but they grew only 25% of the food that was marketed. The remainder was grown by farmers and wealthy landowners on large and efficient estates. Until 1861, when they had been emancipated by Alexander II, most of the Russian peasants had been serfs. The serfs were actually owned by landlords who controlled every aspect of their personal as well as their working lives. They had no rights and were subject to an often brutal discipline.

Life in the Russian countryside – an eyewitness account

Sir Donald Mackenzie Wallace, who travelled through Russia in the 19th century, wrote about the Peasant Communes. In this passage he describes the job of the Commune Elders, elected officials who collected taxes, and the working of the Village Assembly – the meeting of heads of families which decided the Commune's business.

1 'The more laborious and well-to-do peasants . . . try to escape election as office-bearers, and leave the administration in the hands of the less respectable members. Not infrequently a Commune Elder trades with the money he collects as taxes; and sometimes,
5 when he becomes insolvent, the peasants have to pay their taxes a second time. The Village Assemblies have become worse than they were in the days of serfage. Communal affairs are sometimes decided by a noisy majority; and certain Communal decisions may be obtained by "treating the Commune" – that is to say by
10 supplying a certain amount of Vodka.'

Some questions:

(1) Mackenzie-Wallace uses the word 'laborious' in line 1 in a way in which a modern writer might not use it. Can you tell, by reading the rest of the sentence, what he means by 'laborious'?
(2) If you do not know the meaning of the word 'insolvent' (line 5) see if you can guess its meaning by reading the sentence in which it occurs. Check your guess by looking the word up in a dictionary.
(3) If you have read the section on Landlords and Peasants and the piece by Mackenzie-Wallace carefully you will be able to say whether Mackenzie-Wallace visited Russia in the first half of the nineteenth century or in the second half. Give the reason why you chose the answer that you chose.
(4) What were the 'Communal affairs' (line 7) decided by the Village Assembly? If you are not sure of the answer, re-read the section in this chapter entitled 'Landlords and Peasants'.

Sources
Table comparing U.S.A., U.K. and Russia (p.5) is from Nove, A., *An Economic History of the U.S.S.R.* (Pelican Books, 1972) p. 24. Mackenzie-Wallace extract is from Wallace, Sir D.M., *Russia on the eve of War and Revolution* (Random House, New York, 1961) pp 351–2.

1.2 A peasant woman and her children in Russian Central Asia.

members. Since Communes paid their taxes jointly, their members were unlikely to permit anyone to withdraw because those who remained would then have to pay a larger share of the communal tax bill. The Communes made life easier for those peasants who were inefficient, since they were helped along by their more efficient neighbours.

The estates owned by the nobility and gentry were the most modern and efficient sector of Russian agriculture, but between 1861 and 1914 many such estates were sold off in small lots because their owners could not make a satisfactory profit from them. Most of this land was sold to peasants, who farmed it less efficiently. As the figures on page 5 show, Russia's agricultural output was growing between 1870 and 1913, though the population was also increasing rapidly. By 1900 many of the Tsar's advisers were beginning to question the usefulness of the Commune system. The Communes were supposed to keep rural Russia stable and law-abiding, but peasant riots were becoming more common.

Alexander had arranged for the freed serfs to buy land, though many were not able to buy as much as they needed to support themselves. They were to pay the government for their land in yearly instalments, but many peasants quickly fell behind with these Redemption Payments and got into debt. The freed serfs remained members of Village Communes and were obliged to co-operate with each other in farming and paying their taxes. Individual peasants owned land but decisions about how to farm it were made jointly by the heads of all the households in the Commune, who also elected an Elder to supervise the collection of taxes. The eyewitness account of Commune life on page 3 gives some idea of how inefficient this system was. Some enterprising peasants would have preferred to leave the Commune and farm independently, but they were only permitted to leave with the agreement of their fellow Commune

1.3 The Great Vegetable Market in Moscow.

Facts and figures about Rural Russia

(A) Population of Russia up to 1913

	Total population	Population living in towns
1835	60 185 000	–
1860	74 120 000	6 100 000
1897	125 680 000	18 400 000
1913	159 200 000	28 500 000

(B) Food production up to 1913

	Grain harvest in tons
1870	32 500 000
1900	65 000 000
1913	80 000 000

Russian grain production appears to have increased dramatically in the decades before 1913, but the figures demand a closer look.

(1) How could you use both the sets of figures above (**A** and **B**) to work out a new set of figures that would show whether Russian agriculture was keeping pace with the dramatic growth in the population of Russia? Make the calculation and see what the results are.

(2) How could you use both sets of figures (**A** and **B**) to test whether Russian agriculture was becoming more efficient? Make the calculation and see what the results are.

Two important hints:

Use the 1860 population figures to go with the 1870 grain figures and the 1897 population figures to go with the 1900 grain figures. Assume that one third of the population, excluding those living in towns, is involved in the production of grain.

How Russia compared with other countries

One way of comparing the efficiency of agriculture in different countries is to take the total amount of food of all kinds produced and divide it by the number of workers who produced it. These figures are expressed in millions of calories produced by each male farm worker.

	1860	1910
U.S.A.	22.5	42.0
U.K.	20.0	23.5
Russia	7.5	11.0

(1) Why did the U.S.A. achieve such a great increase in efficiency?
(2) Why was this achievement not shared by Russia?

Only one in five of the peasants could read or write. Their diet was often scanty and unvaried, consisting mainly of rye-bread and potatoes. Whole families occupied one room huts, sometimes sharing their living quarters with their livestock. Epidemic diseases were common. A good harvest meant survival rather than plenty, and a bad harvest meant the danger of starvation. Thousands migrated to Siberia in search of new land or sought jobs in the factories.

Urban workers

Russian industry was developing by the 1880s, but Russia was still far behind advanced countries such as Britain and Germany. Sergei Witte, finance minister from 1892 to 1903, was alarmed by Germany's progress. He feared a war between Russia and Germany, and was determined that Russia should catch Germany up in the field of industrial production.

The skills needed for rapid industrial growth could not be found in Russia. Foreign engineers were encouraged to work there, and Witte relied on foreign investors to supply much of the money to finance industrial growth. The results that he achieved were impressive. By 1900 Russia was producing three times as much iron as in 1890, and more than twice as much coal. The figures accompanying the map 'Industrial Russia' on page 8 show the extent of Witte's success. Despite these impressive rates of growth Russia had not caught up with Germany, and the cost of the growth had been very high. Taxes were increased and this made it more difficult for the peasants to keep up their Redemption Payments. Grain that was badly needed in Russia was exported to earn foreign currency. There was a rapid increase in the number of Russians living in towns and cities.

The new urban working class found that life in the towns was hard. Food prices were high, and many workers lived either in barracks provided by their employers or in home-made shanties.

1.4 A barrack-room for blast-furnace workers. These conditions are typical of those experienced by peasants who moved to Russia's industrial regions in the 1890s.

There was no proper water-supply, no drains, and few doctors or schools. The shanties offered little protection against the severe Russian winters.

The pattern of Russia's industrial growth was a recipe for trouble. Many factories were large, and the fact that they were concentrated in a few cities and regions made it easier to revolutionise the workers. Many enterprises were wholly or partly owned by the state, and workers found themselves in direct conflict with the government when they demanded better wages and conditions. Strikes and riots became more frequent. In 1893 the army was called out 19 times to deal with unrest among the workers. In 1902 it had to be called out 365 times.

1.5 Count Sergei Witte, Finance Minister of Russia from 1892–1903 and Prime Minister 1905–6. He strongly opposed Russia's entry into the First World War, and died in 1915.

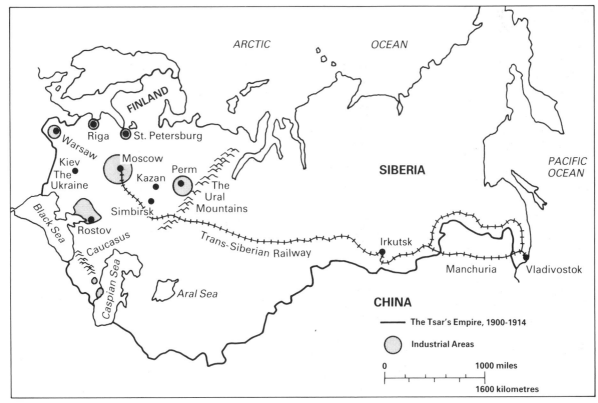

1.6 Industrial Russia.

The number of industrial workers in Russia

1860	565 000
1900	1 692 000
1913	2 282 000

Question: Obviously the number of industrial workers was growing, but were they becoming a bigger section of the total population? Use the figures above and the population figures on page 9 to work out an answer. Use the 1897 population figure for 1900.

Question: If there were 28.5 million people living in towns and cities in Russia in 1913 but only 2.282 million of them were industrial workers, who were all the others? Think about it.

The growth of industrial output

If we use the index number 100 to represent the amount of various items produced in 1890, we can see how much production increased during the Witte era.

	1890	1900
Pig Iron	100	314
Coal	100	269
Steel	100	586
Petroleum	100	275

Did Russia catch up with Germany?

When comparing the industrial performance of two different countries it is important to take into account the difference in size between them. A simple way of doing this is to divide the quantity of material produced by each country by the number of people in that country. The figures in this table are in kilograms per head of population.

	Pig Iron		Coal	
	1890	1910	1890	1910
Germany	14	200	400	3 190
Russia	5	31	–	300

Source
The Industrialisation of Russia (Macmillan Papermac, 1972) p. 76. Comparison with Germany from: Nove, A., *An Economic History of the U.S.S.R.* (Pelican Books, 1972) p. 15.

Population

	Total	Urban
1897	125 680 000	18 400 000
1913	159 200 000	28 500 000

Growth of the Empire's three largest cities

	1850	1900	1910
St. Petersburg	485 000	1 265 000	1 907 000
Moscow	365 000	1 039 000	1 481 000
Kiev	61 000	248 000	447 000

Life in the working class slums of Moscow

'. . . the atmosphere was intolerably stuffy because of the density of the inhabitants. The apartment is damp and unbelievably dirty. In two rooms there is complete darkness. Their ceiling is so low that a tall man cannot stand upright. The plaster is crumbling . . . The stove has collapsed. Legions of cockroaches and bugs. The lavatory is so delapidated that it is dangerous to enter, and children are forbidden to go into it . . . everywhere dampness and dirt. Draughts in every corner; in rainy weather, water on the floor two inches deep.'

What words and phrases in this passage, which describes factory workers' housing in Moscow in 1902, suggest that the writer was a person who lived in a comfortable home and not in one of the slum houses he is describing?

Nationalities

The Russian Empire included many different nationalities, each with its own language and culture. The Great Russians were the dominant nationality because they had, over the centuries, conquered all the others. The Tsar was a Great Russian, as were 44% of his subjects. The other nationalities included civilized peoples such as the Poles, Finns and Ukrainians as well as primitive nomadic tribesmen in Siberia and Central Asia. The table on page 10 shows some of the more important nationalities. There were also religious divisions within the Empire. The Great Russians were mainly of the Russian Orthodox faith, which was the official religion of the Empire. Most of the Poles were Roman Catholics. In the eastern parts of the Empire many people followed the Moslem and Buddhist religions.

Most of the nationalities resented the dominance of the Great Russians and hoped to regain their independence. Since the eighteenth century Russia's rulers had tried to stamp out nationalist feeling by pursuing a policy of Russification – forcing their subjects to speak the Russian language and adopt the Orthodox religion. The Jewish inhabitants of the Empire were subjected to brutal persecution in the form of *pogroms* – campaigns in which the government encouraged people to attack the Jews and their property. Russification, far from stamping out nationalist feeling, served to increase resentment against Great Russian dominance.

The Nationalities of Tsar Nicholas II's Empire

Russia's 1897 Census revealed that the population of the Russian Empire was made up as follows:-

Total:	125 680 000
Great Russians:	55 600 000
Ukrainians:	22 300 000
Byelorussians:	5 800 000
Lithuanians:	1 200 000
Jews:	4 900 000
Poles:	7 800 000
Estonians:	990 000
Latvians:	1 420 000
Germans:	1 780 000
Georgians:	810 000
Tatars:	3 600 000
Kazakhs:	4 000 000
Ten other nationalities:	15 480 000

Using the figures above you can work out just how serious the Tsar's problem of nationalism was. Most national groups resented Great Russian domination and Russification, but some posed a far greater threat than others. The Jews, as a minority persecuted by most of the other nationalities, represented no threat to Great Russian dominance, while the less developed nationalities such as the Tatars, Kazakhs and the ten others grouped together as the last item in the table represented a future rather than a present threat. That leaves eight nationalities distinctly hostile to the Great Russians. Add up their populations. Do they together outnumber the Great Russians? What percentage of the population do they form?

Timeline

Imperial Russia

1894   Tsar Nicholas II succeeds to the throne.

1890s A period of rapid industrialisation, encouraged by the policies of finance minister Sergei Witte.

early A period of economic depression. Strikes and riots by
1900s peasants and workers.

1904   Beginning of the Russo-Japanese War. Birth of Tsarevich Alexis.

1905   Year of Revolution
        Jan: 'Bloody Sunday'.
        Aug: end of the Russo-Japanese War.
        Oct: General Strike. Activities of St. Petersburg Soviet. Tsar issues 'October Manifesto'.

1906   Elections for First Duma. 'Fundamental Laws' issued by the Tsar deprive the Duma of real power.

      Peter Stolypin becomes Prime Minister and embarks on a policy of encouraging the Kulaks to leave the Communes.

1911   Assassination of Stolypin.

      Beginning of a period of economic depression lasting through to 1914. Large-scale strike movement.

1914   Aug: outbreak of First World War.

1915   Tsar appoints himself Commander in Chief. Government in Petrograd now dominated by the Tsarina and Rasputin.

1916   Summer: The Brusilov Offensive.
      Dec: Murder of Rasputin.

1917   'February Revolution' (March 8th onwards) results in the abdication of Tsar Nicholas on March 15th.

      End of the Russian Monarchy.

?1918 Murder of Tsar and his family by the Bolsheviks.

2 The Opposition

Russia had no parliament in 1900 and it was a crime to form a political party or to write or say anything critical of the Tsar. Nevertheless many educated Russians were very critical of Tsarism and even wealthy noblemen played an important part in opposition movements. Some looked to the West, urging that Russia should develop into a constitutional monarchy like Britain or a republic like France. Others thought these western systems were not appropriate to the Russian character and that the Russian people should develop their own system of government.

Zemstvo liberals

Russia's middle class, which included businessmen, shopkeepers and professional people such as doctors, lawyers and civil servants, was very small in number. They knew that Nicholas II had no intention of setting up a parliament with real power, but hoped that he might allow a consultative assembly in which they would have the chance to express their opinions. The Zemstvo system set up by Alexander II in 1864 gave them some opportunity for political activity. The Zemstva were District Councils elected by the better-off citizens in each area, and they had the power to levy taxes and to spend the money on projects such as road improvements and health care. The Zemstva gave middle and upper class Russians the chance to meet and to talk about politics. This small taste of power made them hungry for more, and by the mid 1890s some of them were demanding that the Tsar set up a National Parliament. This demand alarmed Nicholas and his ministers. During the 1890s they limited the activities of the Zemstva. Most Zemstvo members were law-abiding, property-owning citizens who would have supported the Tsar enthusiastically if he had granted them more power.

The Narodniks

Many educated Russians rejected the 'western' ideas of the Zemstvo liberals and believed that the answer to Russia's problems lay with the peasants. The peasants, they believed, were simple, honest and virtuous people. Their Communes were a model of how a fair, sharing community could be run. A peasant revolution would sweep away all the corruption of Tsarist government and purify Russia.

The main obstacle to a peasant revolution was the fact that the great majority of the peasants were deeply loyal to the Tsar. They called him their 'Little Father' and believed that if he only knew about their problems he would sack all the tax-collectors and policemen and make everything better. In the 1870s many educated young Russians went down to the countryside to persuade the peasants that their loyalty to the Tsar was foolish. The attempt failed. The peasants could not understand the long words and complicated ideas of the young enthusiasts from the cities.

The believers in peasant revolution were known as 'Narodniks' or Populists ('Narod' is the Russian word for people). When they found that it was impossible to stir the peasants into rebellion, some of the Narodniks turned to terrorism as a way of undermining Tsarism. They assassinated several government ministers and, in 1881, killed Tsar Alexander II. This violence failed to destroy the Tsars' authority, and during the 1890s Narodnism declined in popularity. The idea of peasant revolution remained attractive and in 1900 a new and better organised party – the Socialist Revolutionaries – was formed. Its members hoped for a peasant revolution which would overthrow the Tsar and establish a peasant republic, and they promised the peasants that the lands of the Tsar, the Church and the noblemen would be distributed amongst them.

Vladimir Ilyich Ulyanov

In 1887 a group of Narodnik students plotted to assassinate Tsar Alexander III. They were caught, tried and hanged. One of them was a young man named Alexander Ilyich Ulyanov. His execution was a terrible blow for his family, especially for his younger brother Vladimir who was seventeen at the time. Vladimir Ilyich Ulyanov is better known by the pen-name that he later adopted – Lenin.

Lenin was born in 1870 in the town of Simbirsk on the river Volga. His father, an inspector of schools, died when Vladimir was fifteen. Vladimir was educated at the local high school where his headmaster, Fyodor Kerensky, noted that he was a brilliant pupil but lonely. He continued his studies at the University of Kazan, but was expelled for joining in a political demonstration. Eventually he was allowed to return to university and in 1891 he qualified as a lawyer at the University of St. Petersburg in the capital city of the Empire.

Lenin had a great admiration for his elder brother but did not share his political beliefs. Among the dead Alexander's books he found a copy of *Capital* by Karl Marx. He read it and found that it contained political theories much more precise than those of the Narodniks.

Karl Marx and Friedrich Engels

Karl Marx was born at Trier in Germany in 1818, but spent much of his adult life in England. He and his friend Friedrich Engels, the son of a Manchester cotton merchant, studied the lives of working people in Britain and developed the system of ideas known as Communism.

2.1 Karl Marx (1818–83), the German-Jewish philosopher and political economist whose book *Capital* analysed the workings of Capitalism.

2.2 Friedrich Engels (1820–95), the friend and collaborator of Karl Marx. Together they wrote the *Communist Manifesto* (1848) and developed the theory of Communism.

Marx and Engels looked on the whole of human history as a struggle between 'haves' and 'have-nots' – a class struggle. In the Middle Ages it had been a struggle between rich barons and poor peasants. In the 19th century it was a struggle between wealthy factory owners and the poor men, women and children who worked for them. Marx and Engels referred to the workers as the 'Proletariat', using a Latin word which means 'people who own nothing but their children'. They referred to the factory owners as 'bourgeois capitalists'. Bourgeois is a French word which originally meant 'town-dweller', and a capitalist is someone who owns 'the means of production' – factories, mines or quarries.

Communism

Marx and Engels believed that wealth and political power go together. In the Middle Ages the kings and landowning barons had run the country. Then wealth and power had passed from the landowners to the factory owners as a result of the Industrial Revolution. This hand-over of power had been a peaceful and gradual process in Britain. Marx and Engels called it 'the Bourgeois Revolution'.

Marx and Engels studied the future as well as the past, and they predicted that another revolution – 'the Proletarian Revolution' – was coming. When it happened, the Proletariat would seize wealth and power from the Bourgeoisie and create a perfect society in which there would be no more struggles between 'haves' and 'have nots' because everyone would be a 'have'. The mines, factories and farms would be owned not by individuals but by the community. That is why Marx and Engels called their idea of a perfect society 'Communism'.

The railway of history

Marx and Engels believed that history was moving towards Communism like a train moving along a fixed track towards a predictable destination. When they studied Britain in the

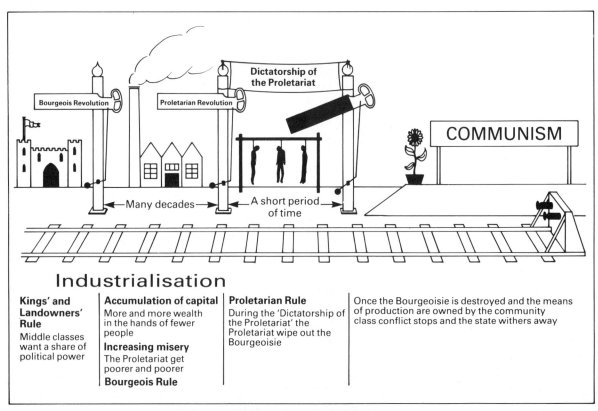

2.3 The Marxist Line – the course of history as Marx and Engels saw it.

mid nineteenth century they noticed that the poor seemed to be getting poorer and that wealth was being concentrated in the hands of fewer and fewer people. They assumed that these trends would continue and that eventually a tiny group of capitalists would own all the means of production and would have to control a huge, angry proletariat. When the proletariat realised the strength of their own numbers they would rise up and stage the Proletarian Revolution.

After the Proletarian Revolution there would be a period called 'The Dictatorship of the Proletariat'. During that time the leaders of the proletariat would use the state-machine (the police, the courts and the civil service) to hunt down and destroy all opponents of Communism. Then, when Communism had been achieved, and when the injustices that made people behave badly had been abolished, there would be no need for the state-machine and it would wither away. The perfect Communist society could only be achieved once the whole world had gone through the revolutionary process.

2.4 This photograph, taken in Nizhni Novgorod (now named Gorki) in the early 1900s, illustrates the extremes of poverty and prosperity in Russia at that time.

These ideas are based on a view of history that is sketchy and selective, and on the assumption that people's behaviour is determined by economic factors. The trends that Marx and Engels detected in mid nineteenth century Britain did not continue. The workers became better off and formed Trade Unions and a political party (the Labour Party) to work for peaceful change. Marx, Engels and their followers found ingenious ways of explaining why history did not follow their predictions. Lenin himself was to make an important contribution to this process of modifying Marx's ideas to meet changed circumstances.

A short-cut to Revolution

It is surprising that the Russians of the 1890s took a strong interest in Marxism. Russia was still ruled by an autocratic monarch and had only just embarked on her industrial revolution. It might be decades before a Bourgeois Revolution happened, and perhaps centuries before the Proletarian Revolution. What gave Lenin and other Russian Marxists hope was that Russia was having her industrial revolution more rapidly because she was able to import money and machinery from other, more advanced countries. In the clash between a new, poor urban working class and the old Tsarist system of government Lenin saw the hope of a revolution.

In St. Petersburg Lenin met other Marxists, and soon impressed them by his cleverness and by the forceful way in which he put forward his views. He was a striking young man, prematurely bald, with ginger hair and a beard. He enjoyed chess and music, though he later gave up these pleasures to devote himself to the study of history, politics and economics and to concentrate on preparing for the revolution.

Among the young Marxists in St. Petersburg was Julius Martov. Like Lenin, he came from a middle class background and had been expelled from university for political activity. Though they disagreed on many issues they were firm friends at this time. Lenin also became friendly with Nadezhda Konstantinovna Krupskaya. Krupskaya was the daughter of an army officer and a convinced Marxist. They met at a Marxist

2.5 Lenin (left) and Julius Osipovich Martov (right) at a meeting of members of the St. Petersburg League for the Emancipation of Labour.

which held its first congress in 1898. The Party was divided on many issues, and most of its leaders were in exile. Some members, 'the Economists', argued that they should throw their energies into the illegal Trade Union movement and work to improve the conditions of the workers. Lenin and Martov were scornful of this idea, pointing out that a worker who is better off will be less likely to want a revolution. There was also an organisation of Jewish Marxists, called the Bund, which was mainly concerned with the problems of Jewish workers.

If the new party was to be strong and united, firm leadership was needed. When Lenin returned from exile in 1900 he travelled to Switzerland to join a group of leading Marxists who had set up a newspaper called *Iskra* ('The Spark'). *Iskra* was printed abroad and smuggled into Russia, and its editors hoped that it would unite all the groups in the Party. Lenin became a member of the editorial board and lived for a time in Germany and London. In 1902 he wrote and published a pamphlet called 'What is to be done?'. The pamphlet attacked the Economists and put forward Lenin's views on how the Party should be organised. This was a subject on which Lenin and Martov disagreed.

Bolsheviks and Mensheviks

meeting which was disguised as a pancake party to avoid attracting the attention of the Secret Police.

The Russian Social-Democratic Workers' Party

At the end of 1895 Lenin and Martov were arrested for their political activities and sentenced to internal exile. This meant that they had to live in a remote part of the Empire for a number of years. The government gave exiles a cash allowance, and it was possible for them to use their time in exile to study and to write. Krupskaya was able to join Lenin in exile in Siberia and they were married in 1898.

While Lenin was in exile his fellow Marxists organised themselves into a political party, the Russian Social-Democratic Workers' Party,

Martov believed that the Party should be a large organisation with as many working class members and supporters as possible. It should be run democratically, and ordinary members should elect the Party's leaders and decide its policies. Lenin was scornful of these ideas. He pointed out that such a party would be easily infiltrated by the Secret Police, and would waste time in debate and argument. The workers were too stupid to understand Marxism or to organise themselves properly, and part-time revolutionaries would achieve nothing. Lenin wanted a small party of full-time revolutionaries under a strong leader. Such a Party would be, in his words, 'the vanguard of the Proletariat', working secretly and effectively to bring about the revolution on behalf of the workers. The extracts on page 17, which are from statements made by Martov and Lenin, illustrate their differing points of view.

The debate on Party organisation

Here are two extracts. One is from a statement made by Lenin and the other from a statement made by Martov. Which is which? Give reasons for your answer.

Statement A

'We are the conscious exponents of an unconscious process. The party organisation is the flywheel which activates party work . . . Let there be organisations with a large membership – they are bound to grow, and the party cannot do without them even though they cannot belong to the party organisation. The more people are entitled to be called party members, the better. We can only rejoice if every striker, every demonstrator who is called to account for his actions can declare that he is a member of the party.'

Statement B

'It is better that ten workmen shall be unable to call themselves party members – what do rank and titles mean to a genuine working man? – than that one chatterbox should have the right to call himself a member . . . What we have to do is to preserve the purity, strength and consistency of our party. We must aim to raise higher and ever higher the importance and dignity of party membership.'

Questions

(1) The author of statement A likens the party organisation to a flywheel. Find out what the function of a flywheel is. Is this an appropriate comparison for the author of statement A to use?
(2) Why was the author of statement B so alarmed at the prospect of having even one party member who was a 'chatterbox'?

Source
Ascher, A. *The Mensheviks in the Russian Revolution,* Thames and Hudson, London, 1976, p. 46. He gives the source: 'Vtoro s'ezd R.S.D.R.P., : Protokoly' (Moscow 1959) pp 270-1, 265, 267-8

The Soviet point of view

This extract is from a life of Lenin published in Russia in 1973. The author, Maria Prilezhayeva, was writing for children and therefore had to be selective in handling the facts. She devotes about a page to the Bolshevik-Menshevik split at the 1903 Congress but does not mention Martov by name.

'The Congress got down to work. Practically from the start a struggle broke out, for there were some delegates who were against Lenin's militant Party Programme. It seemed new and bold to them, and they were frightened by this newness. They argued against Lenin's proposals, but he defended his programme so well that the majority of delegates took his side.

The Congress discussed the Party Rules and Programme. Members of the Central Committee were elected, as was the editorial board of *Iskra.* There was a bitter struggle over every point of the agenda. Lenin made a report that was both concise and convincing. There were 37 sessions in all and Lenin took the floor 120 times. Since the majority of delegates supported Lenin they came to be known as Bolsheviks ('The Majority'). A Bolshevik was a person who stood for a workers' revolution, for a Leninist programme, and for Lenin. Those who had split away from Lenin at the Congress came to be known as Mensheviks ('The Minority'). The Mensheviks stood for abandoning the revolutionary struggle. The Bolsheviks rallied around Lenin.'

When you have read the extract carefully think about the way in which the writer describes the Congress and Lenin's part in it. Which of these three descriptions best fits the author?

A. She admires Lenin and thinks that his views were right.
B. She is neutral towards Lenin, neither admiring him nor criticising him.
C. She dislikes Lenin and disagrees with his views.

Which of the words and phrases that she uses about Lenin made you choose the answer that you chose?

Compare this passage with the section in this book (page 19) which describes the Congress. What are the differences between what the extract says about the Mensheviks and their views and what this book says?

Source
Prilezhayeva, M. *V. I. Lenin – the story of his life,* Progress Publishers, Moscow, 1973, translated by Fainna Glagoleva, pp 55-6

In 1903 the Russian Marxists held a congress in Brussels and London. Their aim was to agree on a new constitution for the Russian Social-Democratic Workers' Party and to resolve the arguments amongst its members. The Congress rejected the ideas of the Economists and the Bund, but then split on the issue of how the Party should be organised. Though a majority of the membership supported Martov, Lenin had a majority among the delegates at the Congress, not least because the Economists and the Bundists, who had withdrawn from the Congress, would have sided with Martov.

Lenin's victory was a hollow one, since the Party immediately split into two rival factions. Lenin's supporters were known as the Bolsheviks (Majority-men) and Martov's as the Mensheviks (Minority-men).

The Tsar and his ministers did not view the Bolsheviks and Mensheviks as a serious threat. Their numbers were small and their leaders were in exile. They sought support amongst the industrial workers who were still a tiny minority of the population. No one in the government would have taken seriously the suggestion that one day Lenin would rule Russia.

3 The 1905 Revolution

An Empire in crisis

By 1900 the Russian Empire was in a state of crisis. Rapid industrial growth had created a new and discontented urban working class. The problem of peasant poverty was acute. Most of the educated upper and middle classes were critical of the Tsar and his methods of government, and resented the laws which prevented them from expressing their opinions. Some believed that violent revolution was the only cure for Russia's ills. Others, the Liberals, still hoped that Nicholas would reform the Empire and establish a parliament.

In the years 1900–4 the crisis grew worse. Bad harvests, inflation and an economic depression resulted in more peasant riots and strikes and protests in the towns. Socialist Revolutionary terrorists assassinated several members of the government. The Tsar's ministers began to fear that the country was on the brink of revolution, and some of them believed that a short, victorious war could save the situation by reviving patriotic enthusiasm and making the people forget their poverty. In 1904 war broke out between Russia and Japan.

The Russo-Japanese War

In the sixteenth century Russia had been a compact kingdom centred on the ancient capital,

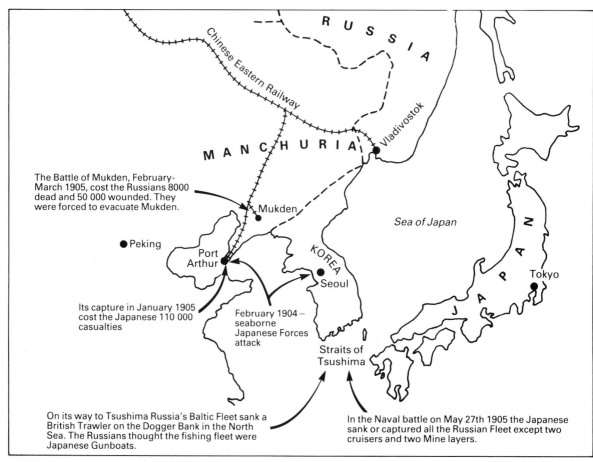

The Battle of Mukden, February-March 1905, cost the Russians 8000 dead and 50 000 wounded. They were forced to evacuate Mukden.

Its capture in January 1905 cost the Japanese 110 000 casualties

February 1904 – seaborne Japanese Forces attack

On its way to Tsushima Russia's Baltic Fleet sank a British Trawler on the Dogger Bank in the North Sea. The Russians thought the fishing fleet were Japanese Gunboats.

In the Naval battle on May 27th 1905 the Japanese sank or captured all the Russian Fleet except two cruisers and two Mine layers.

3.1 The Russo-Japanese war 1904–1905.

Moscow. In the following centuries the Tsars had transformed that kingdom into an Empire stretching from the Baltic to the Pacific. The decline of the Chinese Empire had assisted Russia's eastward expansion, but Japan also had ambitions to conquer Chinese territory, especially the mineral-rich areas of Korea and Manchuria. Russia and Japan became rivals for influence in those areas in the 1890s and by 1904 that rivalry had become so intense that war was unavoidable. The Japanese launched a surprise attack on the Russian base at Port Arthur in February 1904 and the Russo-Japanese War began.

The Tsar was confident of a quick victory, but the war soon revealed that Russia's armed forces were poorly equipped and badly led. Port Arthur fell to the Japanese in January 1905 and the important town of Mukden fell in March of that year. In May 1905 the Russian navy suffered a disastrous defeat at the battle of Tsushima. Far from strengthening the position of the Tsar's government, the war had weakened it.

Bloody Sunday

On Sunday, January 22nd 1905 an orderly crowd of workers and their families marched through the streets of St. Petersburg carrying religious banners and pictures of the Tsar and Tsarina. Their purpose was to present a petition to Nicholas asking for improvements in their working conditions. An extract from the petition is printed on page 23. The Tsar had already left the Winter Palace in the city centre for one of his country residences. When troops and police tried to halt the march, disorder broke out and the troops opened fire. Many people were killed and injured, though the leader of the

3.2 Father Gapon confronts the troops, 'Bloody Sunday', January 22nd 1905.

3.3 Father Gapon. Though Trade Unions were illegal in Russia, the police operated 'tame' unions which, unbeknown to their members, were controlled by police agents. Father Gapon was such an agent, though by 1905 he had developed a sincere sympathy for the plight of the workers and took their side. After 'Bloody Sunday' it was discovered that he had once been in the pay of the police and he was murdered.

demonstration, an Orthodox priest named Father Gapon escaped. The massacre, which came to be known as 'Bloody Sunday', was the beginning of a year of riots, strikes and protests which were to force the Tsar to change his system of government.

In the course of 1905 there were many peasant riots. Units of the armed forces mutinied, and this was particularly alarming to the Tsar since Russia was still at war with Japan. The most famous mutiny occurred in June 1905 when the crew of the battleship *Potemkin* seized control of their ship, threw their officers overboard and after putting in at the Black Sea port of Odessa sought sanctuary at Constanta in Rumania.

In August 1905 the war with Japan came to an end when the Russians signed the humiliating Treaty of Portsmouth in which they agreed to let the Japanese keep Port Arthur and have a free hand in Korea. Soldiers and sailors returned home from the war with stories of hardship and of the incompetence of their officers. Most sections of Russian society were criticising the Tsar's government and demanding change.

The Tsar gives way . . .

As early as March 1905, Nicholas had tried to win back popularity by agreeing to set up a consultative assembly, but the Liberals were no longer satisfied with this and demanded a parliament with real power. In October 1905, in the face of widespread peasant unrest and a General Strike in which even school students and the chorus line of the Imperial Ballet joined, Nicholas finally agreed to more sweeping reforms. He calculated that if he gave the Liberals what they wanted they would turn against the workers and peasants, whose violent and lawless behaviour they feared. Nicholas appointed Witte as Prime Minister and on October 30th they issued the document which became known as 'The October Manifesto'.

The October Manifesto

The Manifesto granted the Russian people basic civil rights which they had not previously enjoyed, such as complete freedom of speech and the right to form political parties. It announced that an elected parliament (the Duma) would be set up, with the power to pass or to reject laws proposed by the Tsar. In theory all males over the age of twenty-five would have a vote, but the system of voting was complicated, and most urban workers were disqualified. The prosperous landowners were given more of a say in the elections than their numbers merited.

Some Liberals accepted the Manifesto with enthusiasm, and became known as 'Octobrists'. Others, including the members of the newly-formed Kadet (Constitutional Democrat) Party viewed the Manifesto with suspicion. They noted that it did not explain exactly how much power the Duma would have, and they did not trust Nicholas II.

. . . and the people respond

The workers and peasants were not satisfied by the Manifesto. Few of them understood it, and it seemed to offer no solution to their immediate problems of poverty, hunger and poor working conditions. They noted that while the Tsar was making concessions, his ministers were using force to break the General Strike. Leon Trotsky,

3.4 Leon Davidovich Bronstein, better known as Trotsky (1879–1940). He played a leading part in the St. Petersburg Soviet of 1905.

Father Gapon and the Police Unions

Trade Unions were illegal in Russia in 1900 but many had been set up. The government decided that it would be safer if there were 'tame' Trade Unions which, unknown to their members, would be under the supervision of the police. This experiment in Police Unions began in 1901. Father Gapon was involved in a Police Union but at the time of Bloody Sunday his working class followers had no idea that he had been in the pay of the police. By 1905 his loyalties had become divided, and he had a real sympathy for the plight of the workers.

The Bloody Sunday Petition

1 'We ask but little . . . reduction of the working day to eight hours, the fixing of wage rates in consultation with us, investigation of our grievances against the factory managements, an increase in the daily rate for skilled men and women to one rouble . . . and the
5 construction of factories in which it is possible to work without risk of death from wind, rain and snow . . . Neither we nor the rest of the Russian people enjoy a single human right, not the right to speak, or to think, or to meet together to discuss our needs, or to take steps to improve our lot. We have been enslaved with the help and co-
10 operation of your officials. Anyone who dares speak up in defence of the interests of the working class and the ordinary people is gaoled or exiled . . . Government by bureaucracy has brought the country to complete ruin, involved it in a shameful war, and is leading further towards disaster. . . Russia is too great and its needs
15 too varied and profuse to be governed by bureaucrats alone. Popular representation is essential. The people must help themselves and govern themselves.'

(1) The workers protested (lines *8–9*) that they did not have the right 'to take steps to improve our lot.' What steps did they want to take to improve their working conditions?

(2) In lines *10–11* the workers accused the Tsar of imprisoning or exiling 'anyone who dares to speak up in defence of the interests of the working class. . . .' Can you, from your study of Chapter 2, think of examples of individuals and groups of people who were punished by the Tsar for that reason? What sort of punishment did they receive?

(3) Which parts of the petition make it clear that the workers had realised that their working conditions would only be improved by changing the way in which Russia was governed?

(4) What do the workers mean by saying (lines *14–15*) that 'Russia is too great and its needs too varied and profuse to be governed by bureaucrats alone'? On the basis of what you have read in Chapter 1, do you think that they were right in saying this?

Source

Bloody Sunday petition is from Floyd, D., *Russia in Revolt*, MacDonald Library of the Twentieth Century, 1969, pp 58–9

Peasant violence in 1905: an eyewitness account

'. . . peasants burned the estates of the landowners, destroying eveything they chanced to get their hands upon – very valuable libraries incomprehensible to them, pictures, porcelain, antique furniture, and even cattle and crops so close to the peasants' hearts. Almost never did the peasants steal, but with a bright flame burned magnificent manors, cattle-sheds, barns and granaries . . . And many landowners fled, without even having time to look back at their beloved homes, on which former generations had lavished so much labor and love.'

Question

Whose side do you think that the writer of this piece was on – the side of the peasants, or the side of the landlords? Which of the words and phrases which she uses give away her point of view? Her identity is revealed at the end of this chapter.

---

a member of the Russian Social-Democratic Workers' Party and one of the leaders of the St. Petersburg workers in 1905 summed it up: 'The Proletariat rejects the police whip wrapped in the parchment of a constitution.' Trouble continued in the cities and in the countryside into December, though with the onset of winter much of the enthusiasm went out of the strike movement and the government was able to restore order by the use of force.

The St. Petersburg Soviet

The unrest of 1905 had not been stirred up or controlled by any of the revolutionary parties, though the Mensheviks did play a part in the workers' movement in St. Petersburg. During the General Strike they suggested that the workers of the city should elect deputies who would form a Council (Soviet). The Soviet became a kind of alternative government. It took charge of the strike. It published its own newspaper *Izvestia* ('News'), and it issued orders to the workers which were generally obeyed. Though the Soviet was dominated by Mensheviks its leading figure, Leon Trotsky, was neither a Bolshevik nor a Menshevik. Like Martov he was Jewish – he had borrowed the Russian-sounding name of Trotsky from a jailer who guarded him in prison. Trotsky, who was born in 1879, was the son of a moderately prosperous farmer. As a student he had been attracted by the ideas of the Narodniks, but he later became a Marxist. After a period of exile in Siberia he joined Lenin in London in 1902 and began to write for *Iskra*. He was a brilliant speaker. In the split of 1903 he sided with Martov on the question of Party organisation, but he did not join the Mensheviks because there were many issues on which he and Martov disagreed.

The Tsar regains control

By early December the workers were growing tired of strikes and protests and Witte judged that it would be safe to suppress the St. Petersburg Soviet. Many of its members were arrested and fifteen of them, including Trotsky, were sentenced to exile in Siberia. Trotsky managed to escape and to make his way out of Russia. The last shots of the 1905 Revolution were fired in Moscow. Here too the workers had formed a Soviet, and in December they called a General Strike and seized control of large areas of the city. Witte ordered troops and artillery to Moscow and the strike was put down with considerable bloodshed and destruction. By the end of the year the Tsar had regained control of the situation.

Nicholas and Witte were determined that the Duma, Russia's new parliament, should have as little power as possible. Witte commented 'I have a constitution in my head, but, as to my heart, I spit on it!' The elections for the Duma were held in March 1906, and only when they were over did the Tsar publish the Fundamental Laws which made clear how much power the Duma would have. The Duma could reject laws proposed by the Tsar, but the Tsar was free to dismiss the Duma and call fresh elections whenever he wished. He also retained the right to appoint and dismiss ministers. In a state of emergency he would be able to govern by decree, without consulting the Duma. He alone had the right to declare a state of emergency. He remained, in fact if not in law, the autocratic ruler of Russia.

The eyewitness account of peasant violence printed on page 24 was written by Mary Stolypin-Bock, whose father, Peter Stolypin, was Governor of Saratov Province in 1905 and earned a reputation for quelling peasant unrest in a firm and ruthless way.

Sources
Peasant violence extract is from: Stolypin-Bock, M. *Memoirs* published in *The Russian Review,* vol 12, no. 3, 1953 in translation and reprinted in *The Russian Revolution of 1917,* ed. von Mohrenschildt, D., Oxford University Press, 1971, p. 20

---

4 The last years of peace

The Duma

The first Duma, in which parties opposed to the Tsar had a majority, met for only seventy-five days before the Tsar dismissed it. During the interval before the second Duma was elected the Tsar issued a number of important laws by decree, and the second Duma was given no opportunity to discuss them. Government pressure during the elections helped to ensure that the Kadets, who had been the largest party in the first Duma, won fewer seats, but the Tsar still did not have a working majority and the second Duma was dismissed after only three and a half months in June 1907. Nicholas then altered the voting system to give more weight to the small class of prosperous landowners. The third Duma, which met in November 1907, was reliable and loyal and was therefore allowed to sit for the normal term of five years.

Peter Stolypin

In July 1906 Nicholas appointed a new Prime Minister, Peter Stolypin. Stolypin had made a great impression on the Tsar by the forceful way in which, as Governor of Saratov Province in 1905, he had dealt with peasant unrest. In his first year as Prime Minister he conducted a vigorous campaign against terrorism. Thousands of terrorists were arrested and executed and the hangman's noose became known as 'Stolypin's necktie'. Stolypin knew that repression alone could not solve Russia's problems. He was aware that industry had grown at a dangerously rapid pace in the 1890s, and he favoured a slower and more natural rate of growth. He also tackled the problem of peasant poverty and unrest. Redemption Payments had already been abolished in 1905, and Stolypin decided to scrap the laws which

4.1 The First Duma in session, 1906.

tied the peasants to the communes. He hoped that the hard-working and enterprising peasants (known as 'kulaks', a Russian word which means 'fist' and was originally applied to village moneylenders) would leave the communes and farm independently. He hoped that they would prosper, buy more land and thus build up larger and more efficient farms on which they would grow more marketable crops. Less efficient and industrious peasants would find it harder to make a living and would be forced to sell their land and work as labourers.

Stolypin believed that the kulaks would be loyal and law-abiding citizens and that they would prevent disorders from breaking out in the countryside. He expressed his faith in them in a famous phrase: 'The government puts its wager not on the drunken and the indigent but on the sober and the strong.'

4.2 Peter Stolypin (1862–1911). When he became Prime Minister in 1906 he said, 'I must carry through effective measures of reform, and at the same time I must face revolution, resist it and stop it.'

4.3 'The sober and the strong' – a group of prosperous peasants and merchants.

How successful was Stolypin?

Stolypin himself believed that twenty years of peace were needed if his reforms were to work, but the outbreak of the First World War in 1914 interrupted the process. Many peasants clung to the communes (in 1915 60% of land in Russia was still being farmed communally) because life was easier in them. As the efficient peasants withdrew from the communes, communal farming became even less productive. The number of kulaks did not increase as rapidly as Stolypin had hoped. By 1915 only 5% of peasant households were making a profit by selling their produce. The limited prosperity of the kulaks was resented by the majority of peasants, and a German professor who toured the Russian countryside just before the First World War commented: 'Stolypin's reform has thrown the torch of civil war into the Russian villages.' Events proved him right. In the peasant unrest of 1917 the kulaks and their property were a target for violence as well as the wealthy landowners.

Stolypin himself was a hated figure. He was murdered in 1911 during a gala performance at the Kiev Opera House, in the presence of the Tsar. The killer was a revolutionary who had also been employed as a police spy.

The pre-war crisis

In 1913 Nicholas and Alexandra celebrated the three hundredth anniversary of the foundation of the Romanov dynasty, but the event aroused little enthusiasm among the people. It happened at a time of economic depression and unrest, and at a time when the Imperial Family had become an object of rumour and scandal.

The years 1911–14 were a time of economic depression in Russia. There was serious rural unrest and the number of strikes in industry rose from 222 in 1910 to 4098 in 1914. The Tsar, fearing a repetition of the events of 1905, used military force to crush the strikes. In a single incident in the Lena Goldfields in 1912 270 workers were killed by troops and a further 250 were injured. The policy of Russification pursued by his predecessors was intensified by Nicholas in the years 1909–14. In 1910 the Finns were deprived of many of the privileges and liberties that they had enjoyed. Decrees were issued banning the use of the Ukrainian language in Ukrainian schools, and nationalist unrest was further provoked in Poland by schemes which sought to deny the Poles a fair representation in the Duma and in their local Zemstva. Nicholas hoped that these measures would stamp out nationalist feelings, but they had the opposite effect.

Rasputin

The scandal that surrounded the Imperial Family concerned a peasant holy man named Grigori Rasputin who, by 1912, had gained a considerable influence at court. Nicholas and Alexandra often followed his advice on important matters of government. From their first meeting with him in 1905 they had been impressed by Rasputin's piety, and they refused to listen to advisers who warned them that Rasputin was a heavy drinker and a womaniser.

4.4 Grigori Rasputin, the peasant holy man who exercised a strong influence over the Russian Imperial Family.

4.5 The Tsarevich Alexis, only son of Tsar Nicholas II. Alexis suffered from haemophilia.

Rasputin's hold on Nicholas and Alexandra had to do with their son, the Tsarevich Alexis, born in 1904. Alexis suffered from haemophilia, an hereditary disorder which hinders the clotting of the blood and makes the slightest scratch or bruise potentially fatal. The Tsar and Tsarina believed that Rasputin had the miraculous ability to cure their son's attacks of bleeding, and this belief made them dependent on Rasputin. Some of the advice that Rasputin gave was sensible – he warned the Tsar that involvement in the First World War would cost him his throne – but his character brought the court into disrepute and further undermined the confidence of the educated classes in the monarchy.

The Revolutionaries

The revolutionary parties were not in a strong position to exploit these difficulties. Their numbers had dwindled since 1905, their leaders were in exile and they spent much of their time arguing among themselves about how to bring about a revolution in Russia. Several attempts were made during this period to re-unite the Bolsheviks and the Mensheviks, but they all failed, largely because Lenin had no wish that they should succeed. He condemned Martov and his supporters for being too soft, referring to them as 'the liquidators of the revolution' because he believed that their democratic methods would prevent the revolution from happening. Martov criticised Lenin for being arrogant and dictatorial, and he also condemned the bank robberies that the Bolsheviks staged as a means of raising funds. The robberies were co-ordinated by a young Bolshevik from Georgia, Joseph Vissarionovich Djugashvili. The son of a poor cobbler, Djugashvili had been sent as a young man to train for the priesthood but had

4.6 Joseph Stalin (1879–1953), seen here as a young man, was one of the few leading Bolsheviks to come from a really poor background.

soon rejected religion in favour of Marxism. He
was later to become famous under an alias –
Joseph Stalin. Both the Bolsheviks and the
Mensheviks put up candidates for the Duma
elections, arguing that the Duma offered an
opportunity to make trouble for the Tsar and
gain publicity for their views. The voting system
and the fact that they were parties which
appealed only to the urban workers prevented
them from winning many seats.

Despite the strikes and riots of the period
1911–4, Lenin doubted whether he would live to
see a revolution in Russia. Other revolutionaries
were more optimistic. Trotsky, for instance,
regretted the outbreak of war in 1914 because he
believed that it had interrupted a promising
revolutionary situation, and that the war would
revive the loyalty of ordinary Russians to the
Tsar.

The origins of the First World War

4.7 Russia and her Western Neighbours in 1914. In the text
Austria-Hungary is referred to as Austria for the sake of
brevity.

The defeat of 1905 at the hands of the Japanese
caused the Tsar and his ministers to concentrate
their attentions on Russia's western frontiers.
After 1906 the Russian army was modernised,
and the Russians abandoned their traditional
defensive policy in the west and prepared to fight
a mobile and offensive war against Austria and
Germany. Russia, Britain and France shared a
common distrust of Germany which, under the
leadership of the Tsar's cousin Kaiser Wilhelm
II, was building a strong navy and demanding a
greater say in world affairs. By 1907 Russia,
Britain and France were united in a defensive
friendship. Russia's quarrel with Germany's
close ally Austria concerned the area of south-
eastern Europe known as the Balkans. Russia
and Austria had been rivals for influence in the
Balkans for several decades. The Russians,
themselves a Slav people, had encouraged the
Slav peoples of the Balkans to throw off Turkish
rule and establish themselves as independent
nations. The Russians had formed a particularly
close relationship with one of these new nations,
Serbia. The Austrians feared the growing
strength of Serbia. There was a large Serb
population within the Austrian Empire, and
these Austrian Serbs would have preferred to
have been citizens of Serbia.

Relations between Austria and Russia
worsened in 1908 when the Austrians annexed
the former Turkish territory of Bosnia-
Herzegovina. The Russians agreed to this
enlargement of Austria on condition that the
Austrians would support Russia's request to be
allowed to bring her warships out of the Black
Sea and through the Straits into the
Mediterranean. Austria made the promise
knowing that the other European Powers would
never agree to Russia's request, and the Russians
felt cheated and humiliated when they refused to
do so. The Tsar was determined not to be
humiliated in future Balkan crises. In the Balkan
Wars of 1912–13 Russia supported Serbia, and
Serbia gained a lot of territory. This alarmed the
Austrians and their German allies, and the
German government began to urge the Austrians
to deal with Serbia. They knew that a war
between Austria and Serbia would probably
develop into a general war involving Germany
and Russia. Many important Germans were
alarmed by the industrial and military progress

that Russia had made since 1890 and argued that they had better fight Russia soon otherwise she would become too powerful to be defeated.

On June 28th 1914 the Archduke Franz-Ferdinand, heir to the Austrian throne, was assassinated at Sarajevo by a Serb terrorist. The Austrians, urged on by Germany, used this as an excuse to provoke a war with Serbia. After the humiliation of 1908, the Russians felt bound to support the Serbs. The complex system of alliances and war plans that existed in Europe in 1914 blew the local conflict up into a major war involving Austria, Germany and Turkey (the Central Powers) on one side and Serbia, Russia, Britain, France and Belgium on the other. For Russia the war began on August 1st 1914.

5 The downfall of the Tsar

Patriotic enthusiasm

The outbreak of the First World War was greeted with great enthusiasm in Russia. Workers attacked the German embassy in St. Petersburg, and the general hatred of things German prompted the government to change the city's name to Petrograd, which sounded more Russian. The majority of the workers and peasants were strongly patriotic. Loyalty to the Imperial Family was revived, and there was a general belief that it would be a short, victorious war. This enthusiasm soon evaporated in the face of high casualties, shortages of munitions, inadequate medical provision for the troops, military defeats and the economic strains caused by the war. The casualty figures – 1 700 000 Russians killed between August 1914 and December 1917 – give an idea of the terrible nature of the conflict.

The revolutionaries and the war

Before 1914 the socialist parties of Europe had pledged themselves not to support wars, believing that it was wrong for workers of different nations to fight each other. When war broke out most socialists supported the governments of their countries, though a minority took a pacifist view and condemned the fighting. Lenin was scornful of both groups, and welcomed the war because he saw that it might lead to the defeat of Russia and to revolution. He spent most of the period 1914–6 in Switzerland, and in 1916 wrote a book, *Imperialism: the Highest Stage of Capitalism,* which explained the war in Marxist terms. Lenin believed that the workers' living-standards had risen (despite Marx's prophecy) because European countries had conquered and exploited overseas colonies. He believed that the First World War was the

5.1 Russian soldiers kneel in prayer as Tsar Nicholas II holds up an icon (holy picture) and blesses them.

result of a desperate competition between the states of Europe to grab colonies and markets.

If Lenin's analysis of the causes of the war was oversimplified, his belief that war would be the midwife of revolution proved, in the case of Russia, to be correct. The Mensheviks were divided on the issue of the war. A majority of them believed in 'revolutionary defensism', and argued that it was necessary to defend Russia against her enemies. Martov, like Lenin, refused to support the war. He hoped it would end in a just peace settlement and a bourgeois revolution in Russia.

The Tsar takes command

1915 was a year of crisis. The Russian armies had failed to win a quick victory in 1914, and German and Austrian counter-attacks had deprived the Russians of much of the territory that they had gained in the early months of the war. The enemy had occupied a large area of Russian Poland. The Russian forces were hampered by a shortage of shells and rifles. In July 1915 the Tsar decided to take personal command of the armed forces in the place of his uncle, the Grand Duke Nikolai. This was a mistake. Nicholas II had little military experience and, as commander, he was held personally to blame for every defeat. His new responsibilities kept him away from Petrograd and the day to day business of government was left in the hands of the Tsarina and Rasputin. The Tsar was bombarded with nagging letters from his wife, who insisted that he follow Rasputin's advice and ignore the suggestions of the Duma. Rasputin, like Nicholas, believed that the Tsar should wield supreme power. Many of the men who were, on Rasputin's advice, promoted to important government positions were incompetent.

The war and the economy

Russian industry grew rapidly to meet the demands of the war. The growth was concentrated in basic industries such as coal, iron, steel and heavy engineering. The government played an important part in setting up new factories, and by 1917 state-owned factories were employing

5.2 Don Cossacks in action on the Eastern Front.

four times as many workers as in 1914. One third of these state-employed workers were concentrated in Petrograd. The war created a large new working class who, like those who had come to the towns in the 1890s, found that their living and working conditions were very poor.

The war also resulted in inflation. By the beginning of 1917 prices were, on average, four times higher than they had been in August 1914. Though the amounts being paid to the workers rose, they were no better off because the food and consumer goods that they wished to buy were in short supply. One of the main causes of inflation was that the government was spending money, at the rate of 28 700 000 U.S. dollars a day, to pay for the war. Inflation wiped out the value of the savings of the middle classes and even affected the peasants. They soon discovered that the money which they were paid when they took their produce to market was worthless, so they sensibly decided to sell less of their produce and to eat more themselves. Rich landowners found that they could no longer afford to pay the higher wages demanded by farm workers so they either stopped cultivating their land or sold it off in small lots to peasants. Either way, efficient farms ceased to produce food for the cities and prices continued to rise. The industrial workers had no savings to fall back on, and could not grow their own food. The peasants resented the high cost of items such as pots and pans, salt and rope. Inflation made all classes of society tired of the war and angry with the government. By the beginning of 1917 there was a food crisis in the cities as a result of inflation and dislocation of the marketing and transport systems. The food crisis was the main cause of the Tsar's downfall.

A government of public confidence

A government of ministers who were changed every few weeks at the whim of a peasant holy man was unlikely to keep the confidence of the people. The Kadets in the Duma began to demand that the Tsar set up a 'government of public confidence' – in other words a government chosen from the members of the Duma and supported by them. For once the Duma politicians and the Army generals found themselves in agreement. By the end of 1916 they had both come to the conclusion that Nicholas II was running the war badly and that Russia would have a better chance of winning it if he abdicated.

The great offensive of the summer of 1916, planned and led by General Brusilov, was intended, like the simultaneous British offensive on the Somme, to relieve the pressure on the beleaguered French positions around Verdun. The Brusilov offensive gained the Russians some ground but no decisive victory and the cost (one million Russian soldiers dead or wounded) was very high. The heavy casualties deepened the disillusionment which ordinary soldiers and junior officers felt towards the High Command – a disillusionment reflected in the eyewitness accounts on page 36. By the autumn of 1916 the troops were war-weary and though they were still prepared to defend Russia, they were reluctant to take part in further offensives. Desertion became more common and Bolshevik agitators began to influence the opinions of the soldiers.

Public criticism of the Tsar and Tsarina grew stronger in the course of 1916. Every one now recalled that Alexandra was of German birth and she was widely, though wrongly, believed to be a German spy. In December 1916 a group of patriotic aristocrats murdered Rasputin in the hope that this would bring the Tsar to his senses. Their deed came too late. The majority of the Duma members and Army generals no longer had any confidence in Nicholas' conduct of the war.

The end of the monarchy

Nicholas' downfall was very sudden. The events described below are often referred to as the 'February Revolution' though by the western calendar they took place in March and the dates given below are all according to the western calendar, which the Russians adopted in 1918.

March 8th 1917:
The Tsar left his palace near Petrograd to return to Army Headquarters. Petrograd was calm though there were some strikes in progress and

Eyewitnesses

Historians, including the present author, often make generalisations such as 'after two years of fighting the Russian soldiers were discontented with the way that their senior officers were running the war.' How do we know? Obviously large-scale desertion and mutiny would be evidence of what ordinary soldiers were thinking. If no such evidence exists we have to rely on written memoirs of the war, and these must be approached with caution. Only the better-educated and more articulate people write things down. Are their views typical? One man's view might be heavily influenced by his personality and political ideas. The experience of a soldier in one part of the front might not be typical.

Historical evidence is more reliable if it can be *corroborated*. Two eyewitnesses who say that the Russian soldiers were disillusioned are worth far more attention than a single eyewitness. In a book such as this there is no space to print a mass of evidence, but these two accounts of morale on the Eastern Front in World War One give you the opportunity to study and to compare two pieces of evidence.

Eyewitness A

'After artillery preparation, we went about a mile forward under heavy enemy gunfire. Once we were within five hundred yards, we were hit, suddenly, by devastating machine-gun and rifle fire that had hitherto been silent. There was the enemy, in solid trenches with great parapets and dug-outs; sitting behind ten or fifteen rows of uncut* wire, waiting for us. We lay on the frozen ground for hours, as the snow drifted down; if we were wounded, there was no help because we were so close to the wire. But behind us, there were artillery colonels and captains of the General Staff, drinking rum tea and writing their reports – "After brilliant artillery preparation our glorious forces rushed forward to occupy the enemy trenches, but were held up by counter-attack of strong reserves." '

* i.e. barbed-wire that the preliminary Russian artillery bombardment had not destroyed.

Source:

Quoted in Stone, N., *The Eastern Front,* Hodder and Stoughton, 1975, p. 224. He attributed it to Kirey, B., *Artilleriya staki i oboroni* (ed. Burov, Moscow, 1926 pp6f).

Eyewitness B

Florence Farmborough, an English girl who before the outbreak of
the war worked as a governess in Russia, was a nurse at the front
during the period of the Brusilov Offensive. This is an extract from
her diary.

Thursday 4th August (1916)

'It was difficult to believe, but the tumultuous firing of the past night
had been all in vain. The enemy's lines were still intact and our men
had been beaten back every time. We had been so sure that now the
tide had turned all would be plain sailing, and that the armies of our
hero, General Brusilov, would have little difficulty in sweeping the
Austrian forces out of Galicia and taking possession of the strategic
passes of the Carpathian mountains. So, here was a deadlock! . . . A
young artillery officer came to seek advice from our medical staff.
He was downcast by the recent catastrophe and criticised the High
Command who, he declared indignantly, were ordering our troops
to continue the advance along the whole South-West Front, no
matter what the cost. "They do not realise how exhausted our men
are," he cried. "In their comfortable armchairs in the base hotels,
with the war-maps stretched before them, they put their finger on a
town – 'Ah', they say, 'that is a grand strategic site. That town must
be seized by our men within the next three days!' And the
command goes forth! And our men, hungry, cold and tired to death,
are expected to spring into action . . . and sweep everything before
them – no matter what the cost." '

Source

Farmborough, F., *Nurse at the Russian Front,* Constable, London,
1974, pp. 225–6

Questions

(1) What facts about the effectiveness of Russian tactics and what
    evidence about the opinions of soldiers and junior officers are
    given in Eyewitness A and corroborated by Eyewitness B?
(2) How can we be certain that Eyewitness A and Eyewitness B are
    not describing events which happened at the same time?

there was only nine days' supply of flour left in the city.

March 8th–9th:
Riots broke out in Petrograd in protest against the war, high prices and food shortages.

March 10th:
The Tsar ordered the soldiers of the Petrograd garrison to suppress the riots. These orders were perhaps unrealistic. The garrison included many new recruits whose discipline was poor and whose sympathies lay with the rioters. Some historians believe that if the officers of the garrison had shown more confidence and determination, the troops might have obeyed them, but the officers did not think so.

March 11th:
The rioting grew worse. Mikhail Rodzianko, the President of the Duma, telegraphed the Tsar to inform him of the seriousness of the situation and to urge him to appoint a Prime Minister who would have popular support. Nicholas commented: 'That fat Rodzianko has sent me some nonsense which I shall not even bother to answer.' He then dismissed the Duma.

The riots grew worse. One of the regiments of the garrison mutinied and joined the rioters.

March 12th:
More regiments mutinied and their soldiers joined the workers in attacking government buildings. The workers and soldiers marched on the Tauride Palace, where the Duma was still meeting despite the Tsar's orders. They demanded to know whether the members of the Duma supported them.

This was a tricky moment for the Duma politicians. Many Kadets feared the workers and were reluctant to side with them. Others argued that if they did not side with the workers and take control of the revolution, then more extreme parties such as the Bolsheviks and Mensheviks would do so. The debate was swayed by a moderate socialist member of the Duma, Alexander Kerensky. Kerensky, who was the son of Lenin's old headmaster in Simbirsk, persuaded the Duma to join the revolution.

March 12th continued:
Rodzianko announced that the Duma was taking over the government of Russia from the Tsar. The workers and soldiers elected a Soviet, which began to meet in the Tauride Palace. Kerensky was one of its deputies.

March 13th:
The Tsar decided to return to Petrograd.

March 14th:
The Tsar, hearing that rebels had blocked the railway line to Petrograd, ordered his train to go to Pskov. Meanwhile Rodzianko got in touch with General Alexeyev, Chief of the General Staff.

Rodzianko and Alexeyev were both worried that the Petrograd mutinies might spread to other regiments. They agreed that the immediate abdication of the Tsar and the setting up of a government of public confidence was the only way to restore order. Rodzianko assured Alexeyev that the Duma would be able to keep order in Petrograd, provided that the Tsar abdicated at once. In Petrograd the Soviet issued 'order no. 1' calling on the soldiers to elect soviets and to refrain from saluting their officers.

5.3 Mikhail Rodzianko (1860–1924), President of the Duma at the time of the Tsar's downfall. Rodzianko died in exile in Belgrade.

March 15th:
Nicholas, now at Pskov, was informed that Alexeyev and the Generals were no longer willing to support him and that he must abdicate. Without army help he could not regain control of Petrograd, so he agreed to abdicate in favour of his son. Later he decided that the boy was not well enough to play any part in public affairs and he abdicated on behalf of Alexis as well, and suggested that his own younger brother, the Grand Duke Michael should be Tsar.

The people might have been prepared to accept Alexis, who was too young to rule, but they were not prepared to accept Michael.

Wisely, Michael abdicated on March 16th. Russia was now a republic, though this was not what either Alexeyev or Rodzianko had intended.

These events took the Bolsheviks and Mensheviks by surprise. Neither party could claim credit for the revolution, which had been a spontaneous uprising of workers and soldiers sick of the war, food shortages and high prices. Martov, Lenin and Trotsky were all abroad when the revolution broke out. A few weeks previously Lenin had gloomily told an audience of Swiss workers that he doubted whether he would 'live to see the coming Revolution'. He was forty-six.

Eyewitness

The extracts below are from the diary of Sybil Grey, a British eyewitness of the revolutionary events in Petrograd in March 1917. Read them carefully and then answer the questions below.

Extract A   Thursday March 8th
On Thursday March 8th a poor woman entered a bread shop on the Morskaia (the Bond Street of Petrograd) and asked for bread. She was told there was none. On leaving the shop, seeing bread in the window, she broke the window and took it. A general, passing in his motor, stopped and remonstrated with her. A crowd collected round them, smashed his motor-car, and, increasing in size, paraded the streets, asking for bread. The same afternoon, on the other side of the river, where the factories are; a factory hand beat his wife on returning home because she had failed to buy him bread. Other women ran in, all saying they had waited hours only to be told 'there is no bread'. The men agreed that it was not the women who were at fault and they must all strike and make demonstrations in the streets – demanding bread.

Extract B   Sunday March 11th
A glorious – sunny – cloudless day. Martial law proclaimed, people warned not to be outside their houses next day. I had all the hospital staff brought over in ambulances. Quite peaceful all the morning, but we were warned that things would happen in the afternoon. At about 3 p.m. I went to the window to look out. It was a glorious day,

people on the bridge were laughing and talking, about ten deep across the road; when looking down Nevsky Prospect I suddenly saw soldiers lie down in the snow ... and fire a volley into the people on the bridge. As soon as the people saw the soldiers lie down, they scattered; but about seven men were caught by the volley while others crawled away on their hands and knees. We had ten casualties brought in, three died (two women) almost immediately. After that the fat was in the fire. Soldiers had fired on the people; nothing now could stop the Revolution.

Extract C   Wednesday March 14th and Thursday March 15th
The Duma Executive is in difficulty as there are three parties: •
  1. For a republic
  2. For compromise with the Emperor, who has not yet answered the telegram.
  3. For his son, with a regency.
Fortunately Rodzianko ... came to an understanding with the extreme left on Tuesday night, and thereby kept control of the people, which saved the situation. ... Not much shooting, but crowds enormous and nervous. There is a bad and uncomfortable feeling. Soldiers saluting officers much less than yesterday.

Questions

(1) What work was Sybil Grey evidently doing in Petrograd at the time of the Revolution? There are clues in extract B.
(2) Some of the incidents that Sybil Grey describes were actually witnessed by her, but she also describes events that she did not see. Make a list of the incidents that you think she actually witnessed. Do you think it likely that she saw the two incidents described in Extract A? Give reasons with your answer.
(3) What evidence is there in extracts A and B of the reasons why the people of Petrograd were in a revolutionary mood?

Questions on Extract C
(4) What was the 'understanding' that Rodzianko had reached with 'the extreme left'? Which organisation represented 'the extreme left' in Petrograd?
(5) Which of the three possibilities mentioned in the extract did Rodzianko himself wish to achieve?
(6) Give a reason why soldiers in Petrograd were 'saluting officers much less than yesterday' (see page 37).

6 The Bolshevik Revolution

The problems of the Provisional Government

The group of Duma members who had played an important part in the downfall of the Tsar appointed themselves as the Provisional or caretaker government of Russia. They intended to govern the country until elections could be held to set up a Constituent Assembly, which would draw up a new constitution for Russia. The war and other problems delayed these elections and by the time that they happened, in November 1917, the Provisional Government had been overthrown by the Bolsheviks.

The Provisional Government was a coalition. At first Kadets, such as Prime Minister Lvov, dominated the government. In May 1917 a few Mensheviks and Socialist Revolutionaries joined them. In July Alexander Kerensky replaced Lvov as Prime Minister and more socialists joined the government.

Because it was provisional and self-appointed the government did not feel that it had the authority to tackle the serious problems that it inherited from the Tsar. Inflation grew worse. By November 1917 prices were ten times as high as they had been at the beginning of the war. Food shortages remained acute. The peasants began to seize land from the church and the aristocracy. The war, which was by now very unpopular, continued. None of these problems could be solved without drastic measures, and the Provisional Government had neither the support nor the confidence to carry such measures out. Nevertheless, it did achieve several constructive reforms. Trade Unions were legalised. Racial and national discrimination were outlawed. Russia became a much freer society. Political prisoners were released and complete freedom of expression was permitted. These measures made it much easier for revolutionary parties such as the Bolsheviks to function.

Dual Power

The Provisional Government had a powerful rival in the form of the Soviets. On March 12th the workers and soldiers of Petrograd had elected a Soviet, and by April 1917 there was a network of Soviets throughout Russia. From the start the Petrograd Soviet functioned as an alternative government. In its famous Order no. 1 published on March 14th, it instructed the armed forces to establish Soviets, to refrain from saluting officers and calling them 'your excellency', and to refuse to obey any order of the Provisional Government unless it was approved by the Petrograd Soviet. Since the Soviet represented workers who ran essential services such as the railways it was possible for it to frustrate the wishes of the Provisional Government by calling them out on strike. Some members of the Provisional Government, such as Kerensky, were also members of the Petrograd Soviet, but the Kadets were not well represented in the Soviet and there were frequent clashes between the Soviet and the Provisional Government.

The Marxists and the downfall of the Tsar

Russian Marxists had to decide where the February Revolution fitted into Marx's pattern of history, and what their attitude to the Provisional Government should be. Most Bolsheviks and Mensheviks believed that what had just happened was Russia's Bourgeois Revolution. Since, according to Marx, the Proletarian Revolution could not happen for a number of years they decided that they had better support the Provisional Government in order to ensure that the Tsar did not regain power. The Imperial Family had been sent to their palace at Tsarskoe Selo near Petrograd, where they were kept as prisoners of the Provisional Government.

Lenin and the April Theses

When the Tsar abdicated, Lenin was still in Switzerland. Desperate to return to Russia, he accepted help and almost certainly money from the Germans. They were willing to help because they knew that he would make trouble for the Provisional Government, and they allowed him to cross Germany in a special train. He reached Petrograd, via Sweden and Finland, late in the evening of April 16th and was given an enthusiastic welcome by his fellow Marxists at the Finland Station.

Everyone assumed that Lenin would, like the majority of the Bolsheviks, support the Provisional Government. He amazed them by asserting that an immediate Proletarian Revolution was possible, and by urging them to work for the rapid overthrow of the Provisional Government and the transfer of power to the Soviets. These views, expressed in a series of speeches, were published as 'The April Theses'. Some Bolsheviks, such as Leon Kamenev, disagreed strongly with Lenin. They pointed out that the Proletarian Revolution could not possibly happen for many years, that the Bolsheviks did not have a majority in the Soviets and that Lenin was cutting them off from all the other Marxist and socialist parties. Despite these attacks Lenin managed to assert his leadership and to persuade the Bolsheviks to accept his ideas. He knew that the Provisional Government was faced with insoluble problems and that the Russian people would soon tire of a government which could not meet their wishes. Lenin summed those wishes up in a famous slogan: 'Peace! Bread! Land!'

Peace

The Soviets demanded an end to the war, calling for 'a just peace without annexations or contributions', by which they meant a peace in which no country would lose territory or be forced to pay reparations. The Provisional Government knew that the Germans would not agree to such terms while they had the upper hand. When the people heard that Foreign Minister Pavel Miliukov had promised Russia's allies that Russia would not make a separate peace with Germany there were riots in Petrograd. Miliukov was forced to resign and on May 18th Prime Minister Lvov invited six Mensheviks and Socialist Revolutionaries to join the government. Kerensky, who had been Minister of Justice, was appointed War Minister.

Kerensky's offensive

In the following weeks Kerensky prepared the Russian Army for an offensive. Given the demoralised state of the troops and the adverse effect on discipline of Soviet Order no. 1 it was a remarkable achievement to restore discipline and to persuade them to attack. The offensive, which began on July 1st, enjoyed some early success but then collapsed in the face of a German counter-attack. The discipline and morale of the army collapsed with it, and the Provisional Government was even more unpopular.

Lenin and the July Days

Lenin saw the events of April–July 1917 as proof of what he had said in April. The continuing war, inflation and shortages of food were causing growing unrest in the towns and the countryside. Because some Mensheviks and Socialist Revolutionaries had joined the Provisional Government, against the advice of Martov and other leaders, both parties were now less popular. The Kerensky Offensive led to a political crisis in Petrograd between July 16th and 18th which became known as the 'July Days'. Soldiers who had been ordered to the front and did not wish to go, radical sailors from the nearby naval base at Kronstadt and workers joined in demonstrations against the government, shouting Bolshevik slogans and calling on the Bolsheviks to seize power.

These events posed a problem for Lenin. He sensed that the time was not yet ripe for the Bolsheviks to seize power, but he knew that if

6.1 St. Petersburg, 1917. Demonstrators scatter as the police open fire.

6.2 Lenin disguised himself in the summer of 1917 by shaving off his beard. This is the photograph from his false identity card.

they did not place themselves at the head of the protests against the Provisional Government they would lose the support of the soldiers and workers. In the end the Bolsheviks did come out on the side of the demonstrators and the results were disastrous. Kerensky was able to turn public opinion against the Bolsheviks by accusing Lenin of being a German agent. Many leading Bolsheviks were arrested and Lenin was forced to go into hiding in Finland. Though the July Days were a serious setback for the Bolsheviks their numbers continued to grow. By the summer of 1917 they had 240 000 members, 91 000 of whom lived in Moscow and Petrograd. In the aftermath of the July Days Kerensky replaced Prince Lvov as Prime Minister.

6.3 Alexander Kerensky (1881–1971). This photograph was taken during his short period as Prime Minister in 1917. After his flight from Russia Kerensky lived mainly in the U.S.A.

The Peasants

Even without any activity by the Bolsheviks, the position of Kerensky's government would have been undermined. In the summer and autumn of 1917 the peasants began to take the law into their own hands. There had already been widespread attacks on kulaks and their property, and many cases in which kulaks were compelled to rejoin communes. By September 1917 the peasants had begun to seize the lands of the Crown, the Church and the aristocracy and to divide them up amongst themselves. The desertion rate in the army rose as soldiers decided to go home and to join the scramble for land. By destroying the efficient sector of Russian agriculture the peasants were making the food shortages even more acute. Inflation made them reluctant to sell food, and the Provisional Government did not have the power to seize it from them by force. In Petrograd and other cities famine was just around the corner and the workers blamed Kerensky's government for the shortages.

General Kornilov

In an attempt to win some support Kerensky held a State Conference in Moscow in August 1917, attended by representatives of the armed forces, industry and all the political parties except the Bolsheviks, who refused to attend. The Conference gave them all the chance to express their views, but Kerensky was unable to persuade a majority of the delegates to support him.

Among the delegates was General Kornilov, the newly-appointed Commander in Chief of the Army. Kornilov wanted to use the Army to close down the Soviets and to restore law and order. Kerensky was attracted by this idea and arranged that Kornilov should bring loyal troops from the front to Petrograd to support the Provisional Government. Kornilov had no intention of supporting the Provisional Government. He was planning to set himself up as a military dictator. Kerensky got wind of this plan and dismissed Kornilov from his command, but Kornilov ignored the dismissal and on September 8th began his advance on Petrograd. Kerensky, who had few troops at his disposal, was powerless to defend the city. The situation was saved by the workers. Railwaymen went on strike and sabotaged the tracks so that Kornilov's troop trains could not approach the city. Bolsheviks infiltrated Kornilov's forces and persuaded many of his troops to desert. A Red Guard of armed workers, organised by the Bolsheviks, prepared to defend Petrograd. Kornilov's offensive collapsed before it got near the city.

The Kornilov plot showed how powerless Kerensky's government was, and revealed that the Bolsheviks were a well-armed and well-disciplined force. During September they began to win majorities in many city Soviets, including those in Petrograd and Moscow. Lenin's slogan 'All power to the Soviets!' was beginning to make sense. The moment for revolution was approaching.

The October Revolution

Russian historians refer to the Bolshevik seizure of power as the October Revolution though by the western calendar it happened in early November. The decision to seize power was taken by the Central Committee of the Bolshevik Party under the leadership of Lenin. On October 23rd they voted in favour of a revolution. Leon Kamenev and Grigori Zinoviev opposed the idea, fearing a repetition of the disastrous July Days. The detailed organisation of the revolution was carried out by Trotsky and the Military Revolutionary Committee of the Petrograd Soviet. Trotsky, who had returned to Russia in May 1917 and had been imprisoned for a short time after the July Days, had joined the Bolshevik Party and was now President of the Petrograd Soviet. While Lenin remained in hiding, Trotsky persuaded the garrison of the Peter and Paul Fortress in Petrograd to hand over the weapons in their arsenal to the Red Guards. From his office in the Smolny Institute, a building formerly used as a girls' school, Trotsky laid plans for the seizure of important government buildings.

Kerensky's government and the people of Petrograd knew that a Bolshevik rising was imminent though they did not know precisely when it would happen. The rising had been timed to coincide with the opening of the All-Russian Congress of Soviets, a conference of elected representatives from Soviets throughout

6.4 St. Petersburg, November 1917. A military patrol car of the Bolshevik Red Guard ready for action on the Nevski Prospect.

6.5 St. Petersburg, November 1917. Soldiers and workers demonstrate in the streets.

Russia. Some Bolsheviks wished to delay the rising until the Congress had had an opportunity to discuss whether it should happen, but Lenin feared that the delegates might not vote in favour of the rising or might waste precious time in lengthy discussions.

There was little that Kerensky could do to stop the Bolsheviks. During the night of November 6th–7th the Red Guards began to take control of important locations such as the railway stations, the telephone exchange and government buildings. Early on the morning of the 7th Kerensky slipped out of the city, intending to go to the front and raise a force of loyal troops with whose support he hoped to regain control of Petrograd. By the evening of the 7th, when the All-Russian Congress of Soviets began to meet, the Red Guards controlled most of the city. The Provisional Government was meeting in the Winter Palace guarded only by officer cadets and by the Women's Battalion of the Russian Army. The signal for the attack on the Palace was given by the Bolshevik-controlled cruiser *Aurora*, which fired a blank shell from her moorings in the River Neva. Red Guards made their way into the Winter Palace and in the early hours of the morning of November 8th a contingent of them arrested the members of the Provisional Government.

While the revolution was happening all around them, the members of the All-Russian Congress of Soviets debated whether or not the Bolsheviks had acted correctly in beginning the rising without first gaining their approval. The Mensheviks and the right-wing of the Socialist Revolutionaries condemned the Bolsheviks' action, but the Bolsheviks were in a majority. 'Go where you belong,' Trotsky told the Mensheviks, 'To the dustbin of History!' Lenin, who had now emerged from hiding to take control of the situation, was greeted with enthusiasm by the Congress. The Bolsheviks had seized control of the capital.

'Ten Days that shook the World'

John Reed, an American journalist, witnessed many of the important events of the October Revolution and wrote about them in his book *Ten Days that shook the World*.

1   'Towards four in the morning I met Zorin (a Bolshevik) in the outer hall, a rifle slung from his shoulder. "We're moving!" said he, calmly, but with satisfaction. "We pinched the Assistant Minister of Justice and the Minister of Religions. They're down in the cellar
5   now. One regiment is on the march to capture the Telephone Exchange, another the Telegraph Agency, another the State Bank. The Red Guard is out"... On the steps of Smolny, in the chill dark, we first saw the Red Guard – a huddled group of boys in workmen's clothes, carrying guns with bayonets, talking nervously together.
10   Far over the still roofs westward came the sound of scattered rifle fire, where the yunkers (officer cadets) were trying to open the bridges over the Neva, to prevent the factory workers and soldiers from the Vyborg quarter from joining the Soviet forces in the centre of the city; and the Kronstadt sailors were closing them again ...
15   Behind us great Smolny, bright with lights, hummed like a gigantic hive.'

Reed also described how Lenin announced the success of the revolution to the All-Russian Congress of Soviets.

'A short, stocky figure, with a big head set down on his shoulders, bald and bulging. Little eyes, a snubbish nose, wide generous mouth, and heavy chin; clean-shaven now but already beginning to
20   bristle with the well-known beard of his past and future. Dressed in shabby clothes, his trousers much too long for him ... A strange popular leader – a leader purely by virtue of his intellect; colourless, humourless, uncompromising and detached ... but with the power of explaining profound ideas in simple terms ... Now Lenin,
25   gripping the end of the reading stand, letting his little winking eyes travel over the crowd as he stood there waiting, apparently oblivious to the long-rolling ovation, which lasted several minutes. When it finished, he said simply, "We shall now proceed to construct the Socialist order!" '

Questions

(1) Do you think that John Reed approved of the Bolshevik Revolution? Disapproved of it? Or was neutral towards it? Which of the words and phrases that he uses give us clues about his attitude?

(2) In lines *10–14* Reed refers to bridges over the Neva being opened and closed. What does his use of the words 'open' and

'close' suggest about the design of these bridges?

(3) In lines *22–3* Reed describes Lenin as 'a leader purely by virtue of his intellect'. What important ideas had Lenin persuaded his fellow Bolsheviks to follow since his return to Russia in April 1917? How had these ideas contributed to the success of the Bolsheviks in the October Revolution?

Source

Reed, J., *Ten Days that Shook the World,* Penguin, 1977, pp. 87, 128–129

7 The Bolsheviks consolidate their power

The new government

At the end of 1917 the Bolsheviks controlled only a small part of Russia, including Moscow which they seized after fierce fighting on November 15th. They had established a government with Lenin at its head and Trotsky as Commissar (Minister) for Foreign Affairs. The cabinet was called SOVNARKOM (short for Council of People's Commissars) and it included some members of the left-wing of the Socialist Revolutionaries. Lenin did not intend to share power with them for long, but needed their support in dealing with the Constituent Assembly.

The problems facing the new government were enormous. Its survival depended on the willingness of soldiers and sailors to support it. The Bolsheviks had created chaos in order to seize power and now needed to re-establish order quickly. The 300 000 Bolsheviks represented the small working class in a country populated mainly by peasants, but many Bolsheviks naively assumed that Russia would immediately become a workers' paradise in which private ownership of land and factories would disappear, the workers would control industry, and government policy would be decided by democratic discussion in the Soviets. Lenin knew that the Bolsheviks would have to fight a civil war to gain control of the rest of Russia, and that this would involve shelving most of the aims

7.1 Lenin in his office in 1918.

and ideals of communism and creating a ruthless, dictatorial government. Lenin believed that the Communist revolution could not survive in Russia alone, but must be spread to other countries.

Land

One of the first acts of the Bolshevik government was a decree of November 8th 1917 handing over the estates of the crown, church and aristocracy to the peasants. Since the peasants had already seized these lands, the decree simply legalised an existing situation. Some Bolsheviks were angered by it, and argued that since land was part of the means of production it should now belong to the state, not to individual peasants. Lenin sensibly pointed out that 300 000 Bolsheviks were not in a position to deprive 125 000 000 peasants of their land. In February 1918 the government did pass a decree which declared that all land belonged to the state, but they did not attempt to put it into force.

The Constituent Assembly

The Constituent Assembly, elected in November 1917, met in Petrograd on January 18th 1918. Since the majority of voters were peasants it was inevitable that the Socialist Revolutionaries, led by Victor Chernov, would do well in the elections, and the 370 seats that they won gave them an absolute majority. The Bolsheviks had 175 seats and their left Socialist Revolutionary allies a further 40. The Mensheviks only won 16 seats. Non-socialist parties such as the Kadets had already been declared illegal and their members were not allowed to take their seats. Lenin dealt with the Assembly ruthlessly. Armed soldiers and sailors invaded the chamber and closed the Assembly down permanently after it had sat for only one day.

The Peace of Brest-Litovsk

In their Peace Decree of November 8th 1917, an extract from which is printed on page 50, the Bolsheviks called for 'a just, democratic peace', but Lenin knew that a quick peace settlement was essential if the Bolsheviks were to retain power, and that they were in no position to dictate terms to the Germans. He favoured a policy of peace at any price. Some Bolsheviks argued that the war with Germany should continue until the revolution spread to Germany. Trotsky suggested a compromise. The Bolsheviks should begin peace talks with the Germans but spin the talks out. He believed that when the German workers saw how greedy their government was for land and gold, they would rise up in revolt. He believed that the revolution could not survive in Russia alone, and that it must be spread to other countries. His plan was adopted, and peace talks began at Brest-Litovsk in Western Russia in December 1917.

Though the Germans terms were harsh, there were no signs of revolt by the German workers. Lenin urged that the terms be accepted. Trotsky suggested a policy of 'neither peace nor war'. The Russians would reject the terms but refuse to fight. If the Germans attacked, as Lenin believed they would, then surely the German workers would revolt against their war-mongering government? Trotsky's policy nearly led to disaster. The Germans renewed their attack in February 1918 and advanced rapidly on a broad front. On February 23rd the Bolshevik Central Committee decided to adopt Lenin's policy of 'peace at any price' and the talks were resumed.

The Treaty of Brest-Litovsk was signed on March 3rd 1918, and its terms were even harsher than those that the Germans had offered before. The map on page 50 shows the extent of Russia's losses. The surrender of Germany and Austria to the Allies in November 1918 meant that the Treaty was no longer valid, and during the Civil War the Russians were able to regain much of the territory that they had lost at Brest-Litovsk. The left Socialist Revolutionaries resigned their positions in the government in protest against the signing of the Treaty and the government became wholly Bolshevik. During 1918 the Bolsheviks changed the name of their party to the All-Russian Communist Party (Bolshevik), and from now on this will be referred to as the Communist Party.

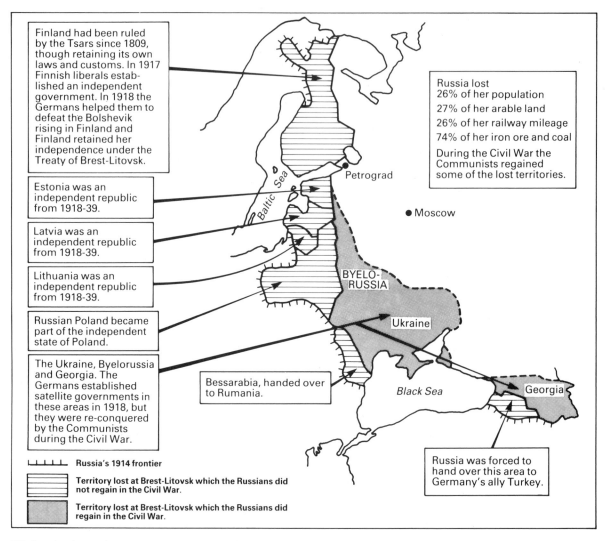

Finland had been ruled by the Tsars since 1809, though retaining its own laws and customs. In 1917 Finnish liberals established an independent government. In 1918 the Germans helped them to defeat the Bolshevik rising in Finland and Finland retained her independence under the Treaty of Brest-Litovsk.

Estonia was an independent republic from 1918-39.

Latvia was an independent republic from 1918-39.

Lithuania was an independent republic from 1918-39.

Russian Poland became part of the independent state of Poland.

The Ukraine, Byelorussia and Georgia. The Germans established satellite governments in these areas in 1918, but they were re-conquered by the Communists during the Civil War.

Russia lost
26% of her population
27% of her arable land
26% of her railway mileage
74% of her iron ore and coal

During the Civil War the Communists regained some of the lost territories.

Petrograd

Baltic Sea

● Moscow

BYELO-RUSSIA

Ukraine

Bessarabia, handed over to Rumania.

Black Sea

Georgia

Russia was forced to hand over this area to Germany's ally Turkey.

└┴┴┴┴┘ Russia's 1914 frontier

Territory lost at Brest-Litovsk which the Russians did not regain in the Civil War.

Territory lost at Brest-Litovsk which the Russians did regain in the Civil War.

7.2 Russian losses by the Treaty of Brest-Litovsk.

The Bolshevik Decree on Peace, November 8th, 1917

This is an extract from the Decree on Peace drafted by Lenin immediately after the successful Bolshevik takeover of Petrograd. Read it carefully and answer the questions below.

'The workers' and peasants' government, created by the Revolution . . . and based upon the Soviets of Workers', Soldiers' and Peasants' Deputies, proposes to all the warring peoples and their governments that they immediately enter into negotiations for a just, democratic peace.

A just or democratic peace, such as the majority of the workers and the toiling classes of the warring countries, exhausted, tormented and ravaged by the war, are yearning for – the sort of peace which the Russian workers and peasants have demanded in most definite and insistent ways since the overthrow of the Tsarist monarchy – this sort of peace, in the opinion of this Government, would be an immediate peace without annexations (i.e., without the seizure of foreign territories and without the forced incorporation of foreign peoples) and without indemnities . . . The Government considers that it would be the greatest of crimes against humanity to continue this war only to determine how the strong and rich nations should divide among themselves the weak peoples they have seized, and it solemnly declares its determination to sign at once a peace putting an end to this war on the terms indicated, equally just for all peoples without exception.'

Source:
Kennan, George F. *Soviet Foreign Policy 1917–41*. D. van Nostrand Inc., Princeton, New Jersey, 1960, pp. 116–17.

Questions

(1) What does the document tell us about the meaning of the Bolshevik slogan 'a just and democratic peace'? If you do not know the meaning of the word indemnities, consult a dictionary.
(2) What did the writer of this decree (Lenin) see as the reason why the other countries involved in the war might wish to continue fighting?
(3) When, earlier in 1917, had the workers and peasants made their feelings on the issue of peace felt by their protests? (see Chapter 6)
(4) How well did the Treaty of Brest–Litovsk match up to the hopes of the Bolsheviks expressed in this document?
(5) If Lenin knew in November 1917 that a quick peace was essential and that the Germans were not likely to agree to 'a just and democratic peace', why did he issue this decree? What was he trying to prove, and to whom?

Civil War

The signing of the peace treaty brought the inevitable civil war closer. Many army units had anti-Communist commanders who, now that they no longer had to defend Russia against Germany, could concentrate on defeating the Communists. The Civil War began in the spring of 1918 and lasted until the end of 1920. During its final stages a war broke out between Russia and the newly-independent state of Poland.

The anti-Communist forces were known as the 'Whites'. White is the traditional colour of monarchists, though not all the Whites were seeking to restore Tsarism. They received help from foreign interventionist powers, including Britain, France, the U.S.A. and Japan, but this help was half-hearted and soon withdrawn. The

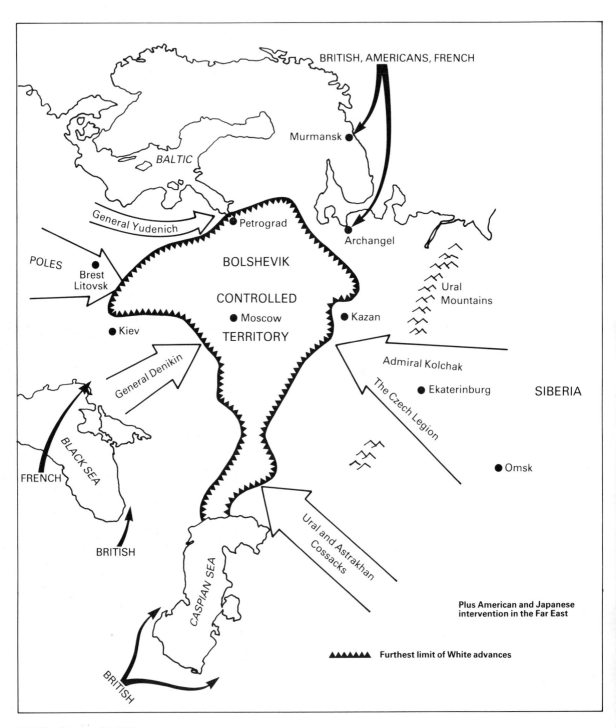

7.3 The Russian Civil War.

interventionist powers were motivated by a fear of Communism and a belief that if it took root in Russia it would spread to their own countries.

The Whites could not agree among themselves about what form of government Russia should have after they had won the Civil War. Some favoured a liberal republic or a military dictatorship, others urged the restoration of the Monarchy. The commanders of the White Armies in the different parts of Russia were unable to co-ordinate their offensives precisely and often quarrelled amongst themselves. The Communists, fighting for survival and defending a central region well served by railways, managed to organise their war effort much better. Trotsky, who became Commissar for War in 1918, formed the Red Army and instilled discipline into it. He toured the fronts in an armoured train, dealing ruthlessly with deserters and incompetents. He and Lenin realised that the Communists needed expert help and advice, and they employed former Tsarist officers such as General Brusilov. Political Commissars were appointed to supervise these officers and were ordered to shoot them if they showed the slightest sign of disloyalty.

7.4 Leon Trotsky harangues members of the Red Army. As Commissar for War Trotsky was the architect of the Bolshevik victory in the Russian Civil War.

The Civil War and War Communism

	1913	1920
Industrial output (1913=100)	100	31
Agricultural output (1913=100)	100	60
Coal production (millions of tons)	29	9
Pig Iron production (millions of tons)	4.2	0.1

Source
Nove, A. *An Economic History of the U.S.S.R.,* Penguin, 1969, Pelican ed. 1972, page 68.

Timeline of the Russian Civil War

ROUND ONE January–February 1918
Success for the Bolsheviks who invaded the Ukraine and defeated the White Armies led by Generals Alexeyev, Kornilov and Denikin.

ROUND TWO March–April 1918
The Bolsheviks lost much land at Brest–Litovsk. The Whites reorganised themselves.

ROUND THREE May–August 1918
Success for the Whites. The Czech Legion, who had been fighting as part of the Imperial Russian Army and were trying to leave Russia via Siberia, attacked the Bolsheviks. Foreign Powers began to send troops to Russia in June.

ROUND FOUR September–November 1918
The Bolsheviks counter-attacked against the Czechs and recaptured Kazan. In November Admiral Kolchak took control of the White forces in the East.

ROUND FIVE Whole of 1919
A number of White offensives (Kolchak's in March, Denikin's in August–October and Yudenich's in September–October) but they were not co-ordinated and the Bolsheviks were able to deal with them separately. The Foreign Powers began to withdraw their forces, a process which was almost complete by December.

ROUND SIX to March 1921
Kolchak captured and executed. Russo-Polish War began in Spring 1920 and ended with the Treaty of Riga, March 1921.

What happened to the Tsar and his family?

After his abdication Nicholas, with his family, was a prisoner first of the Provisional Government and then of the Bolsheviks. Until a few years ago it was generally accepted that the Imperial Family were murdered in the basement of the Ipatiev house in Ekaterinburg by members of the Urals Soviet on the night of July 16th 1918. White forces were approaching the town and the local Bolsheviks feared that they might rescue the Romanovs.

Recent investigations have revealed flaws in this story. It has been pointed out that the 'murder room' was not large enough to contain all the killers and their victims. A British official who investigated the matter in 1918 found evidence that at least some members of the family left Ekaterinburg by train on July 17th. A Russian press report at the time said that only the Tsar had been shot. Yet there was evidence that violence had been committed in the 'murder room'. Had the Romanovs' servants and doctor been killed there? The fate of the family remains a mystery, though the likelihood is that they were murdered by the Bolsheviks at some time during the Civil War. A woman called Anna Anderson said that she was the Tsar's daughter Anastasia and that she had escaped from Russia. She displayed a detailed knowledge of the Tsar's family life.

7.5 The basement room in the Ipatiev house in Ekaterinburg where the Imperial Family may have been executed. Some of the damage shown in the picture was done by White investigators looking for clues to the fate of the Romanovs.

The course of events in the Civil War is shown on the map on page 52. The Whites never managed to attack the Communists on more than one front at exactly the same time. Had they done so, and had the foreign troops remained in Russia longer, the Whites might have won. The war was fought with great ferocity by both sides. Some combatants, such as the Ukrainian Nationalists led by Petlura, fought against both the Whites and the Reds because they hoped to secure independence for their region. Others, like the Green Partisans led by the anarchist Nestor Makhno, fought against both sides because they resented all forms of government.

In May 1920 troops of the newly-independent state of Poland invaded Russia. The Polish leader Pilsudski hoped to gain territory for his country and to weaken Russia by supporting the Ukrainian Nationalists' bid for independence. Later in the year the Red Army counter-attacked, hoping to overthrow Pilsudski's government and establish a communist regime in Poland. The Polish army halted the Russian advance and the Russo-Polish War was ended by the Treaty of Riga in March 1921, neither side having gained a decisive victory.

7.6 Felix Dzerzhinsky, the organiser of the Cheka.

'Iron Discipline' and War Communism

The need to win the Civil War determined the way in which the Communist government of Russia developed. A Secret Police, the Cheka, was established to hunt down Whites. The Cheka, which was run by a Polish-born Communist called Felix Dzerzhinsky, estimated that it executed 6300 people in its first year of activity.

To ensure that the factories produced sufficient war material, Lenin adopted a tough, practical policy known as 'War Communism'. Military discipline was applied in factories, and this 'Iron Discipline' included the death penalty for workers who went on strike or were persistently absent from work. Middle class managers, accountants and engineers – 'bourgeois technical experts', as Lenin called them – were brought in to run the factories, most of which had been placed under workers' control in the months after the revolution, usually with chaotic results. Lenin commented that one man who knew how to run a railway was worth twenty enthusiastic Bolsheviks, but the workers, who had expected that they would be their own bosses under the Communist system, resented having to submit to bourgeois technical experts.

War Communism also involved ruthless treatment of the peasants. Red Guards were sent out into the countryside to seize food for the soldiers and urban workers, and peasants who refused to hand their supplies over were shot. The peasants decided that it was not worth growing food for the Communists to steal and reduced their sowings. The result was an acute food shortage in 1920 and a terrible famine in 1921. It has been estimated that 7 500 000 Russians died of hunger and disease during the Civil War. The towns emptied – workers would not stay where there was no food – and industry declined.

War Communism also involved abandoning the old inflation-ridden currency. For nearly three years wages were paid in food and fuel and trade was conducted on a barter system. Some Communists welcomed War Communism. They believed that Lenin had been too soft on the peasants in the early months of Communist rule, and hoped that the currency would be permanently abolished.

The Civil War ended in a complete Communist victory, but it had turned Lenin's government into a one-party dictatorship.

Though Soviets were still being elected and though, until 1921, other socialist parties such as the Mensheviks were allowed to exist, the cabinet (SOVNARKOM) was composed entirely of members of the Communist Party from 1918. The official head of state was the President (Yakov Sverdlov from 1918–19, and Mikhail Kalinin from 1919–46) but real power lay with the Politburo, a small committee of senior Communists established in 1919 and dominated by Lenin.

7.7 These starving children, victims of the great famine of 1920–1, were photographed at a camp in Samara in October 1921.

Timeline

Bolshevik Russia

1870   Birth of Lenin.

1898   First Congress of Russian Social-Democratic Workers'
            Party.

1903   Brussels–London Congress. Bolshevik–Menshevik split.

1905   Mensheviks with help of Trotsky establish the St.
            Petersburg Soviet.

1917   April: Lenin returns to Russia via Germany and proclaims
            'April Theses', announcing his intention of overthrowing
            the Provisional Government.
            July: 'July Days' rising suppressed by Kerensky. Lenin
            forced into hiding.
            September: Kornilov plot gives the Bolsheviks the
            chance to impress the people with their strength and
            organisation.
            October: The Bolsheviks plan the armed takeover of
            Petrograd.
            November 7th–8th: Bolshevik Revolution in Petrograd.
            December: Beginning of Brest–Litovsk peace talks.

1918   March 3rd: Treaty of Brest–Litovsk.

1918–20   Civil War.

1920–21   Russo-Polish War. Period of acute famine.

1921   March: Kronstadt Rising. Unrest in Tambov. Lenin
            announces N.E.P. at 10th Party Congress.

1922   Lenin taken ill. Zinoviev, Kamenev and Stalin take over
            government.

1924   January: New Constitution of U.S.S.R. comes into force.
                    Death of Lenin.

8 Lenin's last years

By the end of the Civil War, Russia was a ravaged country, suffering the effects of a terrible famine. The industrial growth achieved in the period 1914–7 had been destroyed, partly by the Civil War and partly as a result of the Treaty of Brest–Litovsk. The Communist government had survived, but the policy of War Communism had made it very unpopular.

The Revolution had not spread to other countries, and Lenin realised that for some time Russia would be the only country with a Communist government. A strong army and secret police would be needed to defend that government from external and internal threats, so the dictatorship of the proletariat would have to continue and the achievement of the perfect Communist society would be indefinitely postponed.

Kronstadt and Tambov

In March 1921 sailors at the island naval base of Kronstadt near Petrograd rose in revolt against the Communist government. Their manifesto, an extract from which is printed on page 60, accused the Communists of breaking all the promises they had made in 1917. They had interfered with elections to the Soviets. The Cheka had persecuted members of other socialist parties. The government had stolen food from the peasants. The Communists tried to reason with the Kronstadt rebels but they refused to drop their demands. Units of the Red Army crossed the frozen sea and stormed Kronstadt. Many of the rebels were killed during the fighting or shot after they had been taken prisoner.

Peasants in Tambov Province also rebelled against the government. They attacked and robbed grain convoys, and for several weeks the government was unable to prevent this because they did not have sufficient troops in Tambov. The famine also provoked protests amongst the industrial workers. 77% of Russia's large and medium-sized factories suffered strikes during 1920, though the penalty for striking was death.

The New Economic Policy

Lenin had already realised that a change of policy was needed if the Bolsheviks were to remain in control, and the Kronstadt and Tambov risings reminded the Communists that their rule was not popular. In March 1921, at the Tenth Congress of the Communist Party, Lenin introduced his New Economic Policy (N.E.P.).

N.E.P. meant that the government stopped stealing food from the peasants and permitted them to sell their produce to private traders who became known as 'Nepmen'. This meant that the 'Black Market', which during the Civil War had handled 60% of the food that reached Russia's towns and cities, was legalised. N.E.P. also meant a return to money. The old currency was replaced by a new rouble. Lenin permitted private businessmen to own and run medium-sized and small factories and to make a profit. Only large enterprises – 'the commanding heights of the economy', as Lenin called them – remained in government ownership. Private owners had to obey government rules about wages and working conditions and, like the state-owned factories, had to produce whatever the government directed at a price fixed by the government.

N.E.P. shocked many Communists because it seemed like a step back towards capitalism. Lenin reminded them that Russia badly needed a breathing-space in which to recover from the effects of the Civil War and that the Communists

The Manifesto of the Kronstadt rebels

Read this document, which gives a clear picture of why the Kronstadt rebels were disillusioned with the Communist government, and answer the questions below.

1   'We joined the Communist Party to work for the good of the people and stand for the help of the workers and peasants. Therefore at the present time which our country is surviving, when all our efforts have been trained to the struggle with the misery,
5   cold and hunger, we state that we do not stand for power, but for the interest of the workers . . . The worker instead of becoming the master of the factory, became a slave. He can neither work where he would like, nor can he reject work which is beyond his physical strength. Those who dare to say the truth are imprisoned to suffer
10   in the torture cells of the Cheka or are shot . . . We are fighting for the liberation of the workers from the despotic power of the usurpers. Long live the Soviet power, the true defender of the workers.'

Source
This translation is quoted in Wittlin, T. *Commissar,* pub. Angus and Robertson, page 425.

Questions

(1) Why was it that 'the worker instead of becoming the master of the factory, became a slave?' (lines *6–7*). See Chapter 7.
(2) What was the Cheka? When was it set up, and who was in charge of it? See Chapter 7.
(3) Who is meant by 'the usurpers' (line *11*)? Why had power been taken away from the Soviets in the years 1918–21, and which group of people exercised power during those years? See Chapter 7.

did not have enough officials and troops to run the whole economy themselves. N.E.P. would leave them free to concentrate on important projects such as electrification. He also insisted that Russia must restore trading links with the capitalist countries so that she could import the machinery and raw materials needed to rebuild her economy.

N.E.P. made possible a slow recovery from the catastrophic situation of 1920–21. By 1928 Russian industry was producing roughly the same amount as in 1914. The recovery in food production was more rapid and this brought new problems. Food prices remained fairly low while the price of scarce manufactured goods rose. This 'scissors' crisis meant that the peasants could not afford the tools, pots and pans that they needed. The government passed decrees which slowed down the increase in industrial prices and helped the 'scissors' to close.

Industry and agriculture recover under N.E.P.

	1913	1922	1925	1927/8
Grain harvest (millions of tons)	80.1	50.3	72.5	73.3
Cattle (million head)	58.9	45.8	62.1	70.5
Pigs (million head)	20.3	12.0	21.8	26.0
Coal (millions of tons)	29.0	9.5	18.1	35.4
Pig Iron (millions of tons)	4.2	0.116	1.53	3.2

Source

Nove, A. *An Economic History of the U.S.S.R.,* Allen Lane, 1969, taken from Pelican edition 1972, pp. 94, 110.

The new State

During the Civil War many Mensheviks and Socialist Revolutionaries had fought in the Red Army though they disagreed with Lenin's ideas and methods. Lenin had no intention of sharing power with other socialist parties, and in 1921 he banned the Mensheviks and S.R.s. Most of their leaders were allowed to go into foreign exile. Martov, the Menshevik leader, died of tuberculosis in Germany in 1923, a sad and disillusioned man. By the end of 1921 the Communist Party was the only legal political party in Russia.

Many Mensheviks had joined the Communist Party during the Civil War, and by 1921 Party membership stood at nearly three quarters of a million. In that year Lenin, who had always believed that quality was more important than quantity when it came to Party members, announced a purge in which approximately a third of the members – mostly former Mensheviks and others who did not agree with his views – were expelled from the Party.

Lenin had promised that the various nationalities of the Tsar's former Empire would be allowed to choose whether they wished to be part of a Communist state in Russia or to be independent. Joseph Stalin, himself a Georgian rather than a Great Russian, had been appointed

Commissar for Nationalities. He and Lenin hoped that the nationalities would throw in their lot with the Communists and that the Empire would become a federation of Communist states, in which the nationalities would be allowed local self-government but major issues such as foreign policy and economic planning would be handled by the central government in Moscow. Moscow had become the capital during the Civil War because Petrograd was dangerously close to the front line.

In practice the wishes of the nationalities were ignored. The Communists were not willing to let economically valuable parts of the Empire opt for independence. As they captured areas during the Civil War, they imposed Communist governments on them and turned them into Soviet Socialist Republics. At the beginning of 1924 a new constitution came into force in Russia, replacing the one that the Communists had introduced in July 1918. Russia became the Union of Soviet Socialist Republics (U.S.S.R.). Each Republic had its own government and in matters such as health, justice and education could decide policy without reference to Moscow. In areas such as economic affairs and the activities of the Cheka the Republics had local Commissars who acted under the instructions of a Union Commissar in Moscow. Foreign and Defence policy were entirely in the hands of All-Union Commissars in Moscow.

The Constitution also laid down the basic rights and freedoms of the people and the system of electing local, Republican and All-Union Soviets. All adults were given the vote, with the exception of private traders, monks and lunatics. The system of voting was so organised as to give much more weight to the votes of urban workers, who were more likely to support the Communists, than to the votes of peasants. The Constitution guaranteed freedom of conscience and religion for all, though the Communist Party was opposed to religion and the U.S.S.R. was officially an atheist state.

The parliament of the U.S.S.R. was the All-Union Congress of Soviets, a large body which met for only a few days each year. One of its functions was to elect the Central Executive Committee, a smaller body which met more regularly and had more power. The Central Executive Committee in turn appointed the members of SOVNARKOM, the cabinet of the U.S.S.R.

The Communist Party was organised in a similar way. It too had a large All-Union Congress elected by Party members, and a smaller and more powerful Central Committee. At the top of the Party structure was the Politburo, the small group of senior Communists who decided Party policy. Since the U.S.S.R. was a one-party state and many members of the Politburo were also members of SOVNARKOM, the Politburo was in effect deciding the policy of the government. SOVNARKOM's task was to find ways of carrying that policy out.

The death of Lenin

The pressures of the Civil War and the gunshot wounds that he suffered at the hands of a would-be assassin in 1918 had undermined Lenin's health. From 1922 onwards he suffered a series of strokes which left him partially paralysed and unable to rule the U.S.S.R. He died on January 21st 1924. His body was embalmed and displayed in a glass case in a mausoleum in Moscow's Red Square, which remains a place of pilgrimage for Communists. The city of Petrograd was renamed Leningrad in his honour.

It is interesting that Marxists, who believe that history is shaped by economic forces, should show such reverence towards an individual man. They do so because they recognise the importance of Lenin's impact on Russian history. Nicholas II's reign would have ended in disaster whether Lenin had lived or not, but if there had been no Lenin there would have been no Bolshevik Party and no Bolshevik Revolution. His sense of timing, his realistic approach to problems like the peace talks at Brest–Litovsk and the crisis of 1921 helped the Bolsheviks to gain and to retain power. His ruthless single-mindedness and his ability to modify Marxism to suit the special situation in Russia mark him out from the other Russian socialist leaders. The U.S.S.R. owes its existence and its centralised, authoritarian and repressive system of government to him.

8.1 Lenin and his wife, Nadezhda Konstantinovna Krupskaya, relaxing in Gorki in 1922.

9 Who will succeed Lenin?

Left-wingers v. Right-wingers

The struggle to determine who would succeed Lenin as leader of the Party began even before his death. It was a struggle among the members of the Politburo. The Politburo, like the Party, was divided into left-wing and right-wing groups. Right-wingers such as Bukharin, Rykov and Tomsky approved of N.E.P. and believed that the peasants would only grow enough food to feed the cities if they were allowed to make a profit. 'Enrich yourselves!' Bukharin said to the kulaks.

Such ideas horrified left-wingers like Trotsky, Zinoviev and Kamenev. They saw no place for private profit in a Communist state. They wanted to build up Russian industry rapidly, and they believed that this must involve the government taking control of all farmland and forcing the peasants to work it as paid labourers. That way, they argued, Russian agriculture would soon become modern and efficient enough to feed the cities. Joseph Stalin's aim was to win power for himself, and he was prepared to side with either faction in order to achieve this.

9.1 Nikolai Bukharin (1888–1938) was a strong supporter of N.E.P.

Personalities

Though Zinoviev and Kamenev agreed with many of his ideas, they disliked Trotsky and were determined to prevent his becoming Party leader. Bukharin, Rykov and Tomsky disagreed with Trotsky's ideas. Thus Trotsky had no support in the Politburo, though he was very popular with ordinary Party members and the Army. He was a brilliant, original thinker and the kind of arrogant man who wins arguments rather than friends. Zinoviev, who had been a close friend of Lenin's, was much more popular and many saw him as the obvious successor to Lenin. No one thought of Stalin as a possible leader. He was a grey figure who did important administrative jobs and had the ability to make himself agreeable, but he lacked the brilliance of Zinoviev or Trotsky. During the months after Lenin was taken ill in 1922 Russia was jointly ruled by Zinoviev, Kamenev and Stalin.

Lenin's Political Testament

During his illness Lenin recorded his thoughts about the future of the Party and the characters of its leading members. He instructed his wife to present this document, the Political Testament,

9.2 Grigori Zinoviev (1883–1936), President of Comintern.

'Enormous power'

Stalin had accumulated 'enormous power' because he was willing to do routine administrative work. Apart from his membership of the Politburo he also belonged to the Orgburo, which ran the Party's organisation, and held the posts of Commissar for Nationalities and General Secretary of the Party Central Committee. The latter job gave him enormous power, and the opportunity to build up support for himself by promoting men who agreed with his views.

When Lenin died on January 21st 1924, Trotsky was on sick-leave in the Caucasus. He was absent from the funeral and later claimed that Stalin had deliberately misled him about its date. Stalin stole the limelight, proclaiming his loyalty to Lenin's ideas. In the months that followed he played an important part in building up the cult of Lenin. He knew nothing about the

9.3 Lenin and Joseph Stalin (right). Privately Lenin felt that Stalin was too ambitious and too rude to lead the Communist Party of the Soviet Union.

to the Party Congress after his death. No one except Lenin, his secretaries and Krupskaya knew of the document's existence.

Lenin wrote that the quarrels between Stalin and Trotsky were the main threat to the Party. Trotsky was 'too much possessed by self-confidence' and Stalin 'has accumulated enormous power into his hands, but I am not sure whether he will always use this power carefully enough.' Stalin's lust for power, which was particularly evident in the Civil War, and the abrasive way in which he dealt with Party colleagues alarmed Lenin, who added a postscript to the Testament in 1923:

'Stalin is too rude and this fault . . . becomes intolerable in the office of General Secretary. Therefore I propose to the Comrades to find a way of removing Stalin from that position.'

Political Testament until Krupskaya produced it in May 1924 and explained that Lenin wished it to be presented to the Party Congress. A special meeting of the Central Committee was held to discuss the matter. Stalin was very frightened, but Zinoviev and Kamenev both supported him. They argued that Lenin's fears were groundless and that there was no point in publishing the Testament. The Central Committee accepted their advice and the Testament was suppressed.

A war of words

The struggle with Trotsky during the first year after Lenin's death was a war of words. Trotsky made much of the fact that Zinoviev and Kamenev had both voted against staging the revolution in 1917. Zinoviev, Kamenev and Stalin pointed out that Trotsky had only joined the Bolsheviks in 1917 and that before then he had often attacked Lenin's ideas. Stalin also attacked Trotsky's theory of 'Permanent Revolution'. Trotsky believed that Communism could not survive in Russia alone and that it was essential to spread the revolution to other countries; otherwise the capitalist countries would attack the U.S.S.R. and overthrow Communism. Even if they did not, Russia was too backward a country to build the perfect Communist society on her own. These views were not popular. Attempts at Communist Revolutions in various European countries in the period 1918–23 had all failed and most Party members were weary of war and upheavals and wanted a period of peace and stability for the U.S.S.R.

Stalin argued that it was possible to build a modern, prosperous socialist society in Russia, whatever happened elsewhere. This theory of 'Socialism in one country' matched the mood of most Russian Communists, and was adopted as official Party policy in December 1925. In the debate between 'Permanent Revolution' and 'Socialism in one country' Zinoviev and Kamenev agreed with Trotsky, just as they joined with him in criticising N.E.P., but they were determined to end Trotsky's political career, so they continued to attack him.

Trotsky had no supporters on the Politburo. He loyally obeyed the Party rule which forbade members to make their disagreements public. He even denied the existence of the Political Testament, though by publishing its contents he could have damaged Stalin's reputation. In January 1925 his Politburo colleagues forced him to resign as Commissar for War. Though still a member of the Politburo, he now had little power.

Stalin turns on the Left Opposition

During 1925 the argument about N.E.P. dominated the meetings of the Politburo. Stalin sided with the right-wingers on this issue. This was not because he supported N.E.P., but because he saw a chance of removing Trotsky, Zinoviev and Kamenev from the Politburo. The argument came to a climax at the Party Congress in December 1925, and Stalin and the right-wingers won. The Congress elected several new members to the Politburo, all of whom were loyal to Stalin. With this large majority, he was

9.4 Leon Kamenev (1883–1936). Like Trotsky and Zinoviev he advocated a policy of rapid industrialisation.

able to secure the dismissal of the Left Opposition, as Zinoviev, Kamenev and Trotsky were known, by the end of 1926. In 1927 Trotsky and Zinoviev were expelled from the Party, and Trotsky was exiled to Soviet Central Asia. In 1929 he was exiled from the U.S.S.R.

Stalin turns on the Right Opposition

Having removed the Left Opposition from the Politburo, Stalin then turned on the supporters of N.E.P. By 1928 he had begun to argue in favour of ending N.E.P. and expanding industry even more rapidly than Trotsky had suggested. The Right Opposition, as Bukharin, Rykov and Tomsky became known, were astonished by this change of view, but there was nothing that they could do because Stalin had a clear majority on the Politburo. Bukharin was expelled from the Politburo in 1929 and Rykov in 1930. When Tomsky's term of office ended in the same year, it was not renewed. Stalin was the undisputed leader of the Party and of the U.S.S.R.

Animal Farm

'Animal Farm' by George Orwell tells the story of how the animals on Mr. Jones' farm revolt against Jones and his men and throw them out. Led by two pigs, Napoleon and Snowball, the animals try to create a perfect farm according to the theory of 'Animalism'. When Jones tries to recapture the farm, he and his men are beaten off in the Battle of the Cowshed.

'Animal Farm' is an allegory. The story closely parallels what happened in Russia before, during and after the Revolution. 'Animalism' is Communism, the Battle of the Cowshed is the Civil War, and Mr. Jones represents Capitalism. Here is an extract from the part of the book which deals with events after the Battle of the Cowshed. See if you can work out which important Russian Communists are represented by Napoleon and Snowball, and what the Windmill represents.

'At the Meetings Snowball often won over the majority by his brilliant speeches, but Napoleon was better at canvassing support for himself in between times. . . . Of all their controversies, none was so bitter as the one that took place over the windmill.'

Snowball wanted the animals to put all their efforts into building a windmill to provide the farm with power so that production could be expanded quickly.

'The whole farm was deeply divided on the subject of the windmill. Snowball did not deny that building it would be a difficult business . . . Napoleon, on the other hand, argued that the great need of the moment was to increase food production, and that if they wasted time on the windmill they would all starve to death. . . . Apart from the disputes over the windmill there was the question of the defence of the farm . . . As usual, Snowball and Napoleon were in disagreement. According to Napoleon, what the animals must do was to procure firearms and train themselves in the use of them. According to Snowball, they must send out more and more pigeons and stir up rebellions amongst the animals on the other farms.'

These arguments were finally settled at a Meeting. Snowball made a characteristically brilliant speech in favour of the windmill, but then. . . .

'. . . Napoleon stood up and, casting a peculiar sidelong look at Snowball, uttered a high-pitched whimper of a kind no-one had ever heard him utter before. At this there was a terrible baying and nine enormous dogs wearing brass-studded collars came bounding into the barn. They dashed straight for Snowball, who only sprang from his place just in time to escape their snapping jaws. In a moment he was out of the door and they were after him. . . . Snowball was racing across the long pasture that led to the road. He was running as only a pig can run, but the dogs were close on his heels. . . . Then he put on an extra spurt and, with a few inches to spare, slipped through a hole in the hedge and was seen no more. . . .'

The animals were amazed at the expulsion of Snowball, but there was another surprise in store for them.

'On the third Sunday after Snowball's expulsion, the animals were somewhat surprised to hear Napoleon announce that the windmill was to be built after all.'

Source
Orwell, G. *Animal Farm,* Martin Secker and Warburg, 1945, taken from Penguin Edition, 1974, pp. 43–51.

_____

_____

Timeline

Stalin's Russia

1879   Birth of Stalin at Gori

1905   Stalin's first meeting with Lenin.

1907   Stalin (alias 'Koba') supervises bank robbery attempts to raise funds for the Bolsheviks.

1912   Stalin joins the Bolshevik Central Committee.

1917   Stalin appointed Commissar for Nationalities.

1918–20 Stalin a Political Commissar with the Red Army.

1919   Stalin becomes a member of the Politburo.

1922   Stalin becomes General Secretary of the Party. After Lenin's stroke he, Zinoviev and Kamenev formed the leadership.

1924	Death of Lenin. Stalin saved from disgrace over the 'Political Testament' by Zinoviev and Kamenev.
1925	Trotsky forced to resign as Commissar for War.
1926	'Left Opposition' voted off the Politburo.
1928	Stalin decides to collectivise agriculture. First Five Year Plan begins.
1929–30	Right Opposition expelled from Politburo. Collectivisation begins.
1932	Second Five Year Plan begins.
1934	Murder of Kirov, Beginning of Purges.
1936	Stalin Constitution. Trial of Zinoviev and Kamenev.
1937	Third Five Year Plan begins. Trial and execution of Marshal Tukhachevsky.
1938	Trial of Bukharin and Rykov.
1941	Outbreak of War.
1945	Victory over Germany.
1946	Fourth Five Year Plan.
1948	Death of Zhdanov. 'Leningrad Affair'.
1952	Fifth Five Year Plan.
1953	'Doctors' Plot'. March 5th: death of Stalin.

10 Stalin's economic policies, 1928–41

The need to catch up

Under N.E.P. Russian industry had made up much of the ground lost during the Civil War, but if 'Socialism in One Country' was to be achieved, more rapid growth would be needed. Stalin knew that the U.S.S.R. would only be secure from foreign invasion if it could catch up with the advanced countries of Europe.

When Sergei Witte tried to speed up the growth of Russian industry in the 1890s he was hampered by the inefficiency of Russian agriculture. Stalin faced the same problem. Rapid industrial growth would mean a rapid expansion of Russia's towns and cities, but how was the new urban population to be fed? It was difficult enough in 1927 to ensure that sufficient food got through. Russia could only afford to buy machinery from abroad if she was able to export food. In 1927 and in 1928 the government found that the peasants were less willing to sell their food because the prices offered by the government were very low. Stalin sent squads of men into the Urals region and Western Siberia to seize food from the peasants. This 'Urals-Siberian' method was only partly successful. The government was forced to introduce food rationing in 1928. Industrial growth could not be achieved unless something drastic was done to improve the food supply. At some time during 1928 or 1929 Stalin decided to *collectivise* Russian agriculture.

Collectivisation

A Collective Farm was one in which the peasants pooled their land to form a large unit which they farmed co-operatively. They sold a fixed amount of their produce to the government at a low price and kept any surplus for themselves. Stalin also envisaged State Farms in which the land would belong to the government and the peasants would work it in return for a cash wage. The differences between a Collective Farm (Kolkhoz) and a State Farm (Sovkhoz) are further described on page 71. There were already some Collective Farms in Russia in 1928, but 98.3% of farmland was privately worked by peasants. Some peasants had achieved a modest degree of efficiency and prosperity under N.E.P., and the Communists referred to these as 'kulaks' and encouraged the majority of peasants to regard them with envy and hatred.

Though Stalin intended to collectivise all land, he began by attacking the kulaks. This served two purposes. Firstly it was a warning to the rest of the peasants about what would happen to them if they did not co-operate with collectivisation. Secondly it enabled Stalin to claim that collectivisation was an act of social justice – taking land from 'greedy capitalist kulaks' and making it available to the poor majority of peasants. The 'liquidation' of the kulaks began in 1929. Liquidation meant forcible deportation to Siberia and Central Asia, where they were given the chance to start new farms in these infertile regions. The government did not care that large numbers of them starved to death.

Collectivisation also began in 1929. Peasants who resisted the process – and many fought rather than surrender control of their land – were shot or deported. By March 1930 55% of the land had been collectivised, though in many cases this involved little more than the peasants signing a register. The peasants expressed their resentment by destroying crops, equipment and farm buildings and by slaughtering and eating their livestock. In the face of this chaos, Stalin called a temporary halt to the process of collectivisation. He blamed the chaos, with some justice, on local Communist officials who had

Collective Farms

Stalin set up two types of farm unit. The SOVKHOZ (State Farm) was a farm where land was owned by the State and the peasants worked on it as paid labourers. This meant that they received their wages however badly the farm did. It was felt that the SOVKHOZ was closer to the Communist ideal, but because they were expensive to run, not many farms of this type were established before the Second World War. The goods produced on a SOVKHOZ were simply delivered to the State, and the farm workers bought food from their wages.

The KOLKHOZ (Collective Farm) was much more common, and by 1940 there were approximately 240 000 farms of this type. The average KOLKHOZ contained 76 peasant families who collectively farmed 476 hectares of land, and also enjoyed the use of small private plots. As well as the private livestock owned by its members, the average KOLKHOZ had 60 cattle, 94 sheep and goats and 26 pigs. KOLKHOZ peasants were obliged each year to deliver a fixed quota of food to the State at very low prices. This was an over-riding obligation. The quota had to be delivered even if the KOLKHOZ peasants went hungry. Any surplus would be kept by the peasants.

Collectivisation was supposed to improve efficiency, but the peasants had neither the tools nor the skill to maintain tractors and farm machinery. Stalin established Machine Tractor Stations, and by the end of the 1930s there was one M.T.S. for every forty Collective Farms. Tractors and drivers from the M.T.S. moved from one KOLKHOZ to another, doing the heavy work of ploughing. The M.T.S. also had a political function – making sure that the Collective Farms in its area were obeying the government's instructions. At one time each M.T.S. had a member of the Secret Police on its staff. The Collective Farms were, like the Communes of Tsarist times, a means of keeping Russia's huge peasant population under control. Each KOLKHOZ had a Communist Party official as its Chairman, and his task was to keep the peasants working, to maintain law and order and to educate them in Communist ideas.

become 'dizzy with success' and had tried to achieve collectivisation too quickly. The local officials were frightened of what would happen to them if they failed to collectivise their area swiftly. Slogans such as 'He who does not join a Collective Farm is an enemy of Soviet Power' and 'Either achieve 100% collectivisation in two days or you will be expelled from the Party' spurred them on to greater brutality.

Stalin decided that the peasants should be allowed to own their own houses, a small plot of land on which to grow fruit and vegetables and a few head of livestock. He hoped that these concessions would make the Collective Farm system more popular, but during the lull in collectivisation after March 1930 many peasants left the Collective Farms which they had been compelled to join. Collectivisation began again in 1931, and by 1937 virtually all the farmland in the U.S.S.R. had been collectivised. In the

10.1 The government of the U.S.S.R. issued this picture in 1931 under the title 'We would like to work together'. Most Russian peasants were less enthusiastic to join a Collective Farm than those in this photograph appear to be.

process, five million kulaks were killed or deported and several millions died in the acute famine of 1932–3 which resulted from the peasants' destruction of crops and livestock and the dislocation of production. In November 1932 Stalin's wife, Nadia Alliluyeva, committed suicide. On the evening before her death she had quarrelled bitterly with Stalin, blaming him for the famine, terror and misery that he had brought upon Russia.

The purpose of collectivisation was to improve the efficiency of Russian agriculture. These figures show the extent to which the policy succeeded.

Population of Russia
1913   159 200 000   1939   170 600 000

Grain harvest in millions of tons
1913 80.1   1928 73.3   1933 68.4   1937 97.4

You can calculate for yourselves whether Russia was producing more grain per head of population in 1937 than in 1913. It is important

The Five Year Plans and their results

Population	Total for the U.S.S.R.	Total living in towns and cities
1926	147.0 million	26.3 million
1939	170.6 million	56.1 million

1st Five Year Plan (1928–33) figures in millions of tons

	1927–8	Target	1932–3 actual
Coal	35.4	75.0	64.0
Oil	11.7	21.7	21.4
Pig Iron	3.2	10.0	6.2

2nd Five Year Plan (1932–7) figures in millions of tons

	1932	Target	1937 actual
Coal	64.0	152.5	128.0
Oil	21.4	46.8	28.5
Pig Iron	6.2	16.0	14.5

Expenditure on armaments

	1933	1937	1940
Total spent (millions of roubles):	42 080	106 238	174 350
Defence spending:	1 421	17 481	56 800
Defence spending as a % of total government spending:	3.4%	16.5%	32.6%

Source
Nove, A., *An Economic History of the U.S.S.R.,* Allen Lane, 1969, from Pelican ed. 1972, pp. 191, 225, 227–8.

to remember that the liquidation of the kulaks, the famine and the purges slowed the growth of Russia's population. If a normal rate of growth had been sustained there would have been a further 10 000 000 mouths to feed by 1939.

The expansion of industry

When Stalin decided to speed up the growth of industry he and his advisers drew up a Five Year Plan for growth. The Plan, which was supposed to run from 1928–33, set production targets for Russian industry. It called for a doubling of coal production and of iron and steel output, and a more than threefold increase in the amount of electricity generated. Many of the targets were unrealistically high. The expansion of industry was to be achieved by state ownership. In 1930 private trade and the employment of labour for private profit were declared illegal.

In 1929 Stalin decreed that the targets of the Plan must be met in four years and the shape of the Plan was changed. Originally it had called for

Рукамн отборной, культурной рабочей
молодежи возводится Комсомольск.

10.2 Volunteers from Komsomol (the Young Communist League) at a construction site in the new city of Komsomolsk in Siberia.

growth in all types of industry, but now it concentrated on basic industries such as coal, iron and steel and engineering. Remarkable things were achieved under the first Five Year Plan. Enthusiastic members of Komsomol, the Young Communist League, began to construct new industrial cities such as Magnitogorsk in the Urals and Komsomolsk in Siberia. Other massive projects were achieved by the use of slave labour. People who criticised Stalin's rule were herded into Labour Camps and forced to work on construction projects. They died in their millions, of exhaustion and malnutrition.

The first Five Year Plan achieved its targets in only a few areas of production, such as the manufacture of machinery. In other areas the results were impressive, though the targets were not met. The number of Russians employed in industry doubled during the period of the Plan. In 1932 targets were set for a second Five Year Plan, which was to be completed by 1937. The targets had to be lowered because of the famine and chaos caused by collectivisation. The rise to power of Adolf Hitler, who became Chancellor of Germany in 1933, meant that the Plan was altered to allow for growth in the armaments industry. Some parts of the Plan succeeded. In steel, machine-tools and leather footwear the targets were beaten, though in many other areas of production the results were less than Stalin had hoped for. The Plan was disrupted by the Purges (see Chapter 11) in the course of which

10.3 The first tractor rolls out of the new Stalingrad Tractor Works in 1930. This tractor factory was built as part of the first Five Year Plan.

10.4 A blast furnace worker at the Stalin Metallurgical Plant in the industrial city of Magnitogorsk.

many managers and engineers were killed or deported.

During 1937 a third Five Year Plan was prepared. This Plan was badly disrupted by the need to arm Russia for war with Germany. The Plan was interrupted by the German invasion of the U.S.S.R. in June 1941.

Though targets were rarely met, the overall achievement of the Plans was considerable. In less than a decade Russia had industrialised to the point where she had a chance of surviving a war with Germany, though she was still far behind western countries in terms of technological skill and the production of consumer goods. The human cost of this catching-up process was terrible. Russia in the 1930s was far from being the Communist paradise that Marx and Engels had predicted.

The workers

The new industrial workforce was illiterate, unskilled and undisciplined. Drunkenness and absenteeism were serious problems and many of the new workers returned to their villages once they had had a taste of the poverty and discipline of urban life. Russia needed a skilled, stable workforce and Stalin achieved this by a policy which combined carrot and stick. The carrot consisted of social security benefits, which were not available to collective farm workers, higher wages for skilled workers and medals and honours for those who worked exceptionally hard. The stick was an Iron Discipline reminiscent of War Communism. Workers could only change their jobs with government permission. Absence from work was a crime punishable by imprisonment. Skilled workers were moved to remote areas of the U.S.S.R., thousands of miles from their families. The Trade Unions were controlled by the Communist Party and were used as a means of disciplining the workforce.

In 1931 Stalin decreed that skilled workers would earn three times as much as the unskilled. Even higher rates of pay were given to scientists, engineers and managers. Though cash wages doubled between 1933 and 1937, their value was undermined by inflation and the workers were no better off. The schools, housing, sanitation and health-care in Russia's towns and cities were not adequate to cope with the arrival of millions of new workers from the countryside. Small apartments in city blocks often had several families living in each room. The 1930s was a period of squalor and misery for Russian workers.

The Command Economy

The Five Year Plans are an example of a 'Command Economy'. Stalin and his colleagues decided on production targets and ordered the factories to meet them. The Plans assigned production targets to individual plants. Managers who failed to achieve their targets were executed or deported to labour camps, and fear of this fate encouraged the others to drive their workers even harder or to 'cook the books' and fool the officials of GOSPLAN, the State Planning Agency, into thinking that they had beaten their targets. Anyone who questioned the wisdom of the Plan or asked for a target to be lowered risked being tried as a 'defeatist' or 'saboteur'. Sometimes the Plan itself was irrational. One department of GOSPLAN might call for a massive increase in the output of tractor wheels, while another department would insist on a much smaller increase in the production of the caterpillar tracks to go with them.

Stakhanovites

Workers who produced more than the daily norm that was required of them were rewarded with medals and privileges. The most famous example of this was a coal miner, Alexei Stakhanov. By hard work and the well-planned use of unskilled labour he managed to produce 102 tons of coal in a single shift in 1935. This was fourteen times more than the norm, and Stakhanov became a national hero. A 'Stakhanovite Movement' was set up to encourage other workers to follow his example, and Stakhanov toured the country lecturing on his ideals and methods. Stakhanovism led to a general increase of work norms, and this made the Stakhanovites very unpopular with the workers.

10.5 Alexei Stakhanov, the record-breaking coal miner, explains his methods of working to miners in the Donbass coalfield.

11 Life in Stalin's Russia

The Purges

A widespread political terror accompanied Stalin's economic policies. Its aims were to dispose of people who disagreed with Stalin's views and to frighten the rest of the population into obedience. In December 1934 Sergei Kirov, chief of the Leningrad Communist Party and a member of the Politburo, was assassinated. The murderer was never put on trial, and Kirov's bodyguard died shortly afterwards in mysterious circumstances, facts which have led many historians to allege that Stalin himself planned Kirov's murder. Kirov's death was certainly convenient for Stalin in that it removed one of his main rivals and enabled him to claim that there was a conspiracy against the Party and its leaders. The conspiracy, which Stalin blamed on the exiled Trotsky, provided Stalin with an excuse to arrest, try and execute many senior Communists. In reality there was no conspiracy, but by means of torture, threats to their families and false promises of mercy the Secret Police persuaded many of their victims to confess to crimes that they had not committed. Some of the more important victims made these confessions in public 'show trials', under cross-examination by the State Prosecutor Andrei Vyshinsky. The extract on page 79 illustrates the kind of confession that Vyshinsky was able to draw from his victims. Zinoviev and Kamenev were tried publicly in 1936, Bukharin and Rykov in 1938. Tomsky cheated the Prosecutor by committing suicide before his trial. Of the thirty-three men who had been members of the Politburo since 1919 fourteen were shot on Stalin's orders. By 1939 there were few 'Old Bolsheviks' left to question his authority. The Purges made possible the promotion of younger men who owed their positions to Stalin.

The Terror was not limited to important Party members, but soon developed a life of its own. Frightened men denounced other people to prove their own loyalty or to settle old scores. The slightest criticism of Stalin's government

11.1 Andrei Vyshinsky was chief prosecutor at the Show Trials of the 1930s. Born in Odessa in 1883, Vyshinsky went on to become foreign minister of the U.S.S.R. in 1949, when this photograph was taken.

might result in denunciation, and the great majority of victims received no proper trial. Those who were not executed immediately were sent to Labour Camps in Siberia and the Soviet Arctic, where many of them died of cold, hunger and exhaustion. In order to earn a meagre ration of food the prisoners had to work for up to sixteen hours a day. The sick, who were unable to fulfil this quota, got less food and therefore had less chance of recovery. The Terror was carried out by the Secret Police. Formerly known as the Cheka, G.P.U. and O.G.P.U., the Secret Police was in the period of the Purges part of the Peoples' Commissariat for Internal Affairs (N.K.V.D.). The N.K.V.D. was headed, successively, by Genrikh Yagoda (1934–6), Nikolai Yezhov (1936–8) and Lavrenti Beria (1938–53).

The Show Trials

The main charge against all the victims in the Show Trials was that they had been involved in 'the united centre', a complex conspiracy aimed at the destruction of the Soviet State and its leaders and masterminded by the exiled Trotsky. State Prosecutor Vyshinsky's aggressive and sarcastic interrogations usually concluded with the demand 'that dogs gone mad should be shot – every one of them!' In this extract Vyshinsky is questioning a witness during the trial of 'the Anti-Soviet bloc of Rightists and Trotskyites' in 1938. Isaak Zelensky was a member of the Party Central Committee from 1931–7. As Chairman of Consumer Co-operatives he had been in charge of the distribution of food.

Vyshinsky: . . . but how did matters stand with the butter?

Zelensky: We don't sell butter in the rural districts.

Vyshinsky: I'm not asking what you sell. You were above all selling the main thing – your country. I am speaking about what measures were taken by your organisation to disrupt trade and deprive the population of prime necessities. Apart from sugar and salt, do you know anything concerning butter? . . . Were there any cases when members of your organisation connected with the butter business threw glass into the butter?

Zelensky: There were cases when glass was found in butter.

Vyshinsky: Glass was not 'found', but thrown into the butter. You understand the difference: thrown into the butter. Were there such cases, or not?

Zelensky: There were.

Vyshinsky: For what purpose? To make it 'tastier'?

Zelensky: That is clear.

Vyshinsky: Well, that is organised wrecking and diversive activities. Do you admit that you are guilty of this?

Zelensky: Yes.

Zelensky subsequently received the death sentence.

Source
Conquest, R. *The Great Terror,* Macmillan, London, 1968, pp. 389–90. He attributes it to 'Report of the Court Proceedings in the case of the Anti-Soviet Bloc of Rightists and Trotskyites', English edition, Moscow, 1938.

The results of the Purges

In 1939 the level of the Terror was reduced, though the camps continued to function. Among the millions of victims of the Purges were many of the most gifted and able Soviet citizens. The success of the third Five Year Plan was seriously reduced by the death or disappearance of so many scientists, engineers and factory managers. Every single admiral, three of the five Marshals of the Red Army, a majority of senior officers and roughly half the entire officer corps were purged. They were alleged to have been involved in a plot to overthrow Stalin organised by Marshal Tukhachevsky, who was executed in 1937. As a result of the Purges it was a young and inexperienced group of officers who faced the Germans in 1941. The progress of science was hindered because the government murdered able men and promoted those, like the biologist Lysenko, whose views were in line with Communism. Gifted writers like Isaac Babel and Osip Mandelstam (the subject of the extract on this page) were victims of the Terror.

The assassination of Trotsky

After his exile Trotsky had become an 'unperson' in the U.S.S.R. His name was removed from history books and photographs which showed him in Lenin's company were either destroyed or altered to exclude Trotsky. He knew that his life was in danger, and his villa in Mexico was heavily guarded. The N.K.V.D. recruited a young Communist called Ramon Mercader to kill Trotsky. Mercader posed as a sympathiser and gained access to Trotsky's villa. One day he brought an article that he had written and asked Trotsky's opinion of it. As Trotsky studied the article, Mercader struck him on the head with an ice-pick. Trotsky died of his wounds on August 21st 1940, and Mercader was sentenced to twenty years in prison.

Hope against Hope

In 1934 the Russian poet Osip Mandelstam was arrested for writing a poem which criticised Stalin, 'the Kremlin mountaineer' who '. . . rolls the executions on his tongue like berries.' The intervention of friends saved him from execution, though the physical and psychological torments that he endured at the hands of the N.K.V.D. drove him to attempt suicide. Having completed a period of internal exile he returned to Moscow in 1937, only to be arrested again in 1938 and sentenced to five years hard labour. His brother was notified of his death later that year. Mandelstam's devoted wife Nadezhda tried to discover from survivors of the Labour Camps how her husband had met his end. One of the survivors that she questioned was a physicist whom she refers to as 'L'. This is what 'L' was able to tell her.

'The transit camp was terribly overcrowded, and there was no room for the new prisoners, who were ordered to settle down in the open air between two rows of barracks. . . . When the rains started, there were great fights to get places in the barracks. By this time 'L' had been selected "elder" of a group of sixty men. His only duty had been to distribute the bread ration . . . but when the rains started, they demanded that he find a roof for them. 'L' suggested that they see whether there was still any room in the lofts above the barracks . . . They soon heard about a loft which was occupied by five criminals, though there was room for three times as many. 'L' and some of his comrades went to reconnoiter. . . .'

'L' made friends with the leader of the criminals, Arkhangelski, though the members of 'L''s group refused to move into the loft.

'Once Arkhangelski invited 'L' to come up to the loft and listen to some poetry. 'L' was not frightened of being robbed, since for months he had been sleeping in his clothes and his rags would not have tempted even a camp thief. All he had left was a hat, but in the camps this was of no value. Curious as to what sort of poetry it might be, he accepted Arkhangelski's invitation. The loft was lit by a candle. In the middle stood a barrel on which there was an opened can of food and some white bread. For the starving camp this was unheard of luxury. People lived on thin soup of which there was never enough – what they got for their morning meal would not have filled a glass. . . . Sitting with the criminals was a man with a gray stubble of beard, wearing a yellow coat. He was reciting verse which 'L' recognized. It was Mandelstam. The criminals offered him bread and the canned stuff, and he calmly helped himself and ate. Evidently he was only afraid to eat food given him by his jailers. He was listened to in complete silence and sometimes asked to repeat a poem.'

Later 'L' lost touch with Mandelstam, and he was unable to tell Mandelstam's widow of the precise circumstances of her husband's death. This is how Nadezhda Mandelstam concludes her book 'Hope against Hope'. Her grief and uncertainty stand for the grief and uncertainty of millions of Russians.

'All I can do, therefore, is to gather what meager evidence there is and speculate about the date of his death. As I constantly tell myself, the sooner he died, the better. There is nothing worse than a slow death. I hate to think that at the moment when my mind was set at rest on being told in the post office that he was dead, he may actually have been still alive and on his way to Kolyma. The date of his death has not been established. And it is beyond my power to do anything more to establish it.'

Question

'L' gives quite a lot of detail about what life was like in the Transit Camp where he met Mandelstam, though it should be remembered that life in the Transit Camps was not as grim as life in the Labour Camps. What details does 'L' provide about the prisoners' diet, living conditions and accommodation?

Source
Mandelstam, N. *Hope against Hope,* tr. Max Hayward, Collins and Harvill Press, London, 1971, pp. 391–2, 396–7.

The Stalin Constitution

In 1936 Stalin announced a new Constitution, which had been drafted by Bukharin, to replace that of 1924. Its function was to give the U.S.S.R. the appearance of a free and democratic country. The All-Union Congress of Soviets (the parliament of the U.S.S.R.) was replaced by a two-chamber assembly called the Supreme Soviet. One Chamber, the Soviet of the Union, had a deputy for every 300 000 voters and thus included a large number of Great Russian deputies. The other Chamber – the Soviet of Nationalities – had an equal number of deputies from all Republics, thus giving the other nationalities a greater representation. The Supreme Soviet met for only a few days in the year. Elections, held every four years, were not contested. Candidates had to be approved by the Communist Party. Monks, who had been disqualified under the 1924 Constitution, were given the vote. Power remained in the hands of small groups of men such as SOVNARKOM and the Politburo. The Constitution guaranteed freedom from arrest without trial and undertook to make paper and printing equipment available to the workers so that they could freely publish their ideas. These promises were not kept.

The Arts in the U.S.S.R.

Creative artists such as writers, composers and painters were expected to be loyal servants of the State. The tasks that they were expected to perform were laid down by Andrei Zhdanov, a hard-line Communist who had succeeded Kirov as head of the Leningrad Communist Party. Anyone who wished to publish their writings had to belong to the Union of Soviet Writers, established in 1932. At its first congress in 1934, Zhdanov ordered the members to concentrate on the theme of Socialist Realism. Their novels, poems and plays must be about ordinary people and their working lives. They must be optimistic in mood, emphasising the ways in which Russia had improved. There was to be no place for fantasy, or for the kind of writing that explores the private feelings of the writer and his characters. Zhdanov condemned such writing as 'bourgeois individualism'. The novel 'How the Steel was tempered' by Nikolai Ostrovsky is an example of Socialist Realism. An extract is printed on page 83. Painters and sculptors were also expected to produce Socialist Realism – statues of muscular and determined men and women building dams, and paintings of happy peasants queueing up to join a Collective Farm.

It is easy to see how Socialist Realism could be imposed on writing and the visual arts. Music, unless in the form of opera, ballet or programme music, is much more abstract. Yet even here Stalin and Zhdanov imposed their ideas about what was good socialist art. They disliked much modern music because it was complicated and above the heads of ordinary people. They criticised composers who copied foreign styles or worked to complex sets of rules which ordinary people could not understand. They wanted music which was cheerful and optimistic and which reflected the heroism of the Russian people in the past and the present.

Religion in the U.S.S.R.

Marx was an atheist who condemned religion as 'the opium of the people' because he thought that priests taught people passively to accept the miseries of this life in the expectation of better things in the hereafter. The new Bolshevik government confiscated the property of the Russian Orthodox Church because its clergy had supported the Tsarist system. During the Civil War active persecution of Christians began, and in 1926 the League of Militant Atheists was formed to organise anti-religious propaganda. By a decree of 1929 Stalin forbade the churches to engage in any other activity than worship. He believed that education would quickly wipe out religious belief, but compulsory lessons in atheism in Russian schools, the arrest of many clergymen and the persecution of those who persisted in attending church did not produce the rapid results that he had expected. In the 1937 Census fifty million Russians are believed to have indicated that they still held religious beliefs. These findings were not published, and the leaders of the League of Militant Atheists were purged for their failure. By 1939 there were only a few hundred functioning churches in the U.S.S.R. These were allowed to operate so that the government could claim that the 'freedom of conscience' clauses in the 1936 Constitution were being honoured.

Socialist Realism

This is an extract from 'How the Steel was tempered', the autobiographical novel by Nikolai Ostrovsky which was first published in 1934. The hero, Pavel Korchagin, comes from a poor home and is an enthusiastic member of Komsomol, the Young Communist League. The first love of his life, Tonya Tumanova, is from a middle class background.

1 'Pavel sought at once to draw Tonya into Komsomol activities. He began by inviting her to attend a meeting of the town's Komsomol. Tonya agreed to go, but when she emerged from her room where she had been dressing for the meeting Pavel bit his lips in chagrin.

5 She was very smartly attired, with a studied elegance which Pavel felt would be entirely out of place at a Komsomol gathering.

This was the cause of their first quarrel. When he asked her why she had dressed up like that she took offence. "I don't see why I must look like everyone else. But if my clothes don't suit you, I can

10 stay at home."

At the club Tonya's fine clothes were so conspicuous among all the faded tunics and shabby blouses that Pavel was deeply embarrassed. The young people treated her as an outsider, and Tonya, conscious of their disapproval, assumed a contemptuous,

15 defiant air. . . .

That evening marked the beginning of the end for their friendship. With bitterness and dismay Pavel watched the break-up of a relationship that had seemed so enduring. Several more days passed, and with every meeting, every conversation they drifted

20 farther and farther apart. Tonya's cheap individualism became unbearable to Pavel. Both realized that a break was inevitable. . . .

Today they had met in the Kupechesky Gardens for the last time. The paths were strewn with decaying leaves. . . . Tonya looked at the golden shafts of sunlight and said with deep sadness: "Is our

25 friendship going to fade like that dying sun?" Pavel, who had been feasting his eyes on her face, knitted his brows sternly and answered in a low voice: "Tonya, we have gone over this before. You know, of course, that I loved you, and even now my love might return, but for that you must be with us. I am not the Pavlusha I was

30 before. And I would be a poor husband to you if you expect me to put you before the Party. For I shall always put the Party first, and you and my other loved ones second." '

Questions

(1) What does Pavel mean when he thinks about 'Tonya's cheap individualism' (line *20*)?
(2) What does Pavel mean by ' "You must be with us" ' (line *29*)?
(3) 'How the Steel was tempered' is a classic in the U.S.S.R. and has been used as a set book in schools because the hero, Pavel, displays qualities and ideas which are highly valued by Communists. Which of these qualities and ideas are demonstrated in the passage above?

11.2 This sculpture, entitled 'A worker and a woman collective farmer', dates from 1937, and is the work of Vera Mukhina. It typifies the kind of art of which Stalin and Zhdanov approved.

Humour in Stalin's Russia

Here are a few jokes that were current in the U.S.S.R. during Stalin's era.

A flock of sheep was stopped by frontier guards at the Russo-Finnish border. "Why do you wish to leave Russia?" the guards asked them. "It's the N.K.V.D.," replied the terrified sheep. "Beria's ordered them to arrest all elephants." "But you aren't elephants!" the guards pointed out. "Yes," said the sheep, "But try telling that to the N.K.V.D."

One day a professor of Music at a Russian university, angered at the ignorance of his students, complained to a friend who was an officer in the N.K.V.D.: "My students can't even say who wrote the opera 'Eugene Onegin' ". Two days later the N.K.V.D. officer stopped him in the street. "We arrested your students," he told the Professor, "and twelve of them have already confessed that they wrote 'Eugene Onegin' themselves."

Stalin complained to a colleague that his office in the Kremlin was infested with mice and that traps and poison had failed to get rid of them. "No problem," the colleague replied. "Just declare that your office is a Collective Farm. Half the mice will run away and the other half will die of starvation."

Source
Based on jokes printed in the article cited below. Russian Review, Vol. 16, no. 3, July 1957, *The Anecdote – Unrationed Soviet Humour,* by W. H. Chamberlin.

12 Soviet foreign policy, 1918–41

Isolation

Many countries had officially recognised the Provisional Government in 1917, but when the Bolsheviks seized power most countries broke off relations with Russia. The rest of the world regarded the new Communist state with distrust and several countries intervened on the White side in the Civil War (see Chapter 7). Russia had no say in the Versailles Peace Conference and did not join the League of Nations.

Comintern and the Foreign Ministry

The Russian Communists' success in staging a revolution gave them considerable authority over Communist parties in other countries. In 1919 the Russians established a world-wide organisation of Communist parties called the Third International, or Comintern. Grigori Zinoviev was its first president. Through Comintern the Russians insisted that Communist parties in other countries follow their instructions. Comintern was supposed to work for world-wide revolution by organising and financing strikes, protest movements and subversion throughout the world. Its leaders often forgot this purpose and worked instead for the short-term interests of the U.S.S.R. If Russia wished to establish friendly relations with a country, Comintern would order the Communists in that country to abandon their subversive activities.

At the end of the Civil War Russia badly needed foreign money, machinery and skills with which to rebuild her shattered industries. Alongside the revolutionary activities of Comintern the Russians operated a more conventional foreign policy through their Foreign Ministry. The Foreign Ministry worked to persuade other countries officially to recognise the government of the U.S.S.R. and to trade with Russia. Sometimes Comintern and the Foreign Ministry found themselves pursuing conflicting aims.

Treaties and Trade Agreements

The Foreign Ministry's first major success was a Trade Agreement signed with Britain in 1921. In 1924 the British officially recognised the Communist government of the U.S.S.R., though the Americans withheld recognition until 1933. Russia did not join the League of Nations until 1934. By 1922 the Russians had signed Trade Agreements with most neighbouring countries, including Finland and Poland.

Germany, like Russia, was an outcast nation. The Versailles Treaty of 1919 had forced her to accept the blame for the outbreak of the First World War, to pay reparations, to give up territory and to accept strict limits on the size and scope of her armed forces. These limitations drove the German government to seek an alliance with the U.S.S.R. In April 1922 the Russians and the Germans signed the Rapallo Pact, which established normal relations between the two countries, and opened up trading and investment links between them. Secretly the Russians agreed to allow the Germans to manufacture in the U.S.S.R. the armaments forbidden to them by the Versailles Treaty, and to train airmen and tank crews there.

The Far East

The Communists had inherited from the Tsar's government a fear of Japan, an increasingly powerful nation with ambitions to conquer more of the Chinese mainland. The Russians had no wish to see Japan victorious in China but were afraid that the Japanese might attack Eastern Siberia. China was in a state of chaos in the early 1920s. The feeble government in Peking had no authority over most of the country. The south was dominated by the Chinese Nationalists (Kuomintang or Guomindang) whose aim was to unite the country and transform it into a modern, liberal democracy. Large areas of the country were controlled by independent warlords. The Chinese Communist Party, established in 1921 was, like the Chinese proletariat, very small. Most of Russia's leaders favoured supporting the Kuomintang, who seemed to have the best chance of uniting China. This made sense in Marxist terms. A Kuomintang victory would amount to a successful bourgeois revolution in China and a step on the long road towards the Proletarian Revolution. In 1923 Comintern signed an agreement with Dr. Sun Yat-sen, the Kuomintang leader. Moscow ordered the Chinese Communists to co-operate with the Kuomintang in every way, and gave the Kuomintang military assistance.

While Comintern was building this relationship with the Kuomintang, the Russian Foreign Ministry officially recognised the Peking government in 1924. They hoped that the Peking government would acknowledge Russia's claim to Sinkiang Province and Outer Mongolia, both formerly part of the Chinese Empire.

Comintern's policy backfired on the Russians. After Sun's death in 1925 the leadership of the Kuomintang passed to Chiang Kai-shek, who hated and distrusted the Communists. In 1926 Chiang began his Northern Expedition, whose aim was the conquest of northern China. In the course of the expedition, Kuomintang forces turned on the Chinese Communists in Shanghai in 1927 and massacred large numbers of them. The expedition resulted in the overthrow of the Peking government. Russia broke off relations with the Kuomintang and cut off aid to China.

Stalin and the rise of Hitler

By the early 1930s Russia's valued relationship with Germany was turning sour. The rise of the Nazi Party and the aggressively anti-Communist and anti-Russian views of its leader Adolf Hitler should have alarmed Stalin, but Stalin seriously underestimated the Nazi menace. He believed that if Hitler gained power he would not hold it for long and that his downfall would pave the way for a Communist revolution in Germany. He ordered the German Communists to ignore the Nazi threat and to concentrate their attacks on the Social-Democrats, their main rival in the

struggle for working class support. This division amongst his left-wing opponents made it easier for Hitler to come to power in 1933. Within a few weeks he outlawed the Communist Party and arrested most of its leaders. Stalin began to take the Nazi menace more seriously and to look for allies.

In 1934 Russia joined the League of Nations and in 1935 she signed agreements with France and Czechoslovakia under which Russia and France promised to support the Czechs against German aggression. Through Comintern Stalin instructed the Communist Parties of Europe to co-operate with other socialist parties and form Popular Front governments to combat the spread of fascism. The Russians gave military aid and advice to the Republicans in the Spanish Civil War of 1936–9, though this did not prevent the victory of General Franco and the Spanish fascists.

Stalin was anxious to persuade the nations of Western Europe that the U.S.S.R. was not a sinister power bent on world revolution, and that she might be a valuable ally against Germany. In Britain and France, the two countries with which Stalin most wanted to secure alliances, suspicion of Communism remained much stronger than suspicion of Nazism. The Munich Crisis of 1938 demonstrated the lengths to which Britain and France would go to avoid conflict with Germany. Neither country was prepared to support the Czechs when Hitler demanded the Sudetenland. Stalin was not invited to the Munich Conference and did not intervene when Hitler occupied the Sudetenland (October 1938) or the rest of Czechoslovakia (March 1939). The 1935 agreements only committed the Russians to supporting the Czechs if the French did so as well.

The betrayal of Czechoslovakia by Britain and France confirmed Stalin's belief that the British and French wanted to encourage Hitler to attack the U.S.S.R. and hoped that such a war would weaken both Germany and Russia. The cartoon on page 88 illustrates this point of view. Stalin decided to seek an agreement with Germany. It was clear that Poland would be Hitler's next target and Stalin did not believe that Britain and France would try to stop him. In August 1939 Russia's Foreign Minister Vyacheslav Molotov

12.1 'On the Great European Road'.

Source
Cartoon 'On the Great European Road', which is reproduced in Richards, Denis, *An Illustrated History of Modern Europe*, Longmans, 1977, page 317.

Study this cartoon, which was published in the U.S.S.R. in the 1930s, and answer the questions below. The left hand arm of the signpost reads 'Western Europe' and the right hand arm reads 'U.S.S.R.'

Questions
(1) Which European country is represented by the car and its occupants? The occupants are all important leaders of that country? Can you name any of them?
(2) The two policemen standing by the signpost are both prime ministers of important Western countries. Which countries do they represent?
(3) Why are the policemen trying to direct the car down the right hand road? Which Western policy, greatly resented by the Russians, does the cartoon illustrate?
(4) When do you think the cartoon was published? Give reasons to support your answer.

had talks with the German Foreign Minister, Ribbentrop, in Moscow. The result of these talks was the German-Soviet Non-Aggression Pact (also known as the Molotov-Ribbentrop Pact) which was announced on August 23rd 1939. The published part of the Pact said that Germany and Russia would remain neutral towards each other, but there were secret clauses in which Russia and Germany agreed to divide Poland between them. The Germans also gave the Russians a free hand to conquer Bessarabia, Latvia, Lithuania, Estonia and part of Finland –

all territories which the Russians had lost at Brest–Litovsk.

Both Russia and Germany benefited from the Pact. The Germans were able to invade Poland in September 1939 without any doubts about Russia's reactions. They were confident that they would soon over-run Russian-occupied Eastern Poland in a future war. Stalin knew that Russia was not yet ready for war with Germany. The Pact gave him valuable time in which to continue his armaments programme.

12.2 August 1939. Soviet foreign minister Molotov signs the Nazi-Soviet Non-aggression Pact while German foreign minister Ribbentrop (standing left) and Stalin (standing middle) look on.

Soviet conquests in Eastern Europe

The Russians attacked Poland on September 17th 1939 and occupied the eastern parts of the country. By the end of 1939 they had forced Latvia, Lithuania and Estonia to accept Soviet garrisons on their territory, and these countries were incorporated into the U.S.S.R. in August 1940. In November 1939 the Russians offered the Finns certain territories in exchange for Finnish territory that was of strategic importance in the defence of Leningrad and Murmansk. The Finns rejected the offer, and at the end of November Soviet troops invaded Finland. At first Finnish resistance was very effective, but the Russian offensive of February 1940 forced the Finns to ask for peace. The Treaty of Moscow, signed in March 1940, gained the Russians more territory than they had originally asked for. Russia was expelled from the League of Nations for attacking Finland.

Bessarabia was occupied by Soviet forces in June 1940.

Stalin had hoped that the Germans would become bogged down in a lengthy war with Britain and France, but by the end of 1940 Hitler had conquered much of Western Europe and only Britain remained in arms against him. In December 1940, after abandoning plans to invade Britain, Hitler ordered his generals to prepare for an attack on the U.S.S.R. Stalin continued to co-operate with the Germans, mistakenly calculating that the more friendly he was, the longer they would delay their attack. Communists in German-occupied Europe were ordered not to take part in resistance activity. German naval vessels were allowed to use the Russian port of Murmansk and the Russians continued to supply Germany with vital raw materials, while denouncing the Churchill government for its 'warmongering' and 'unreasonable' attitude.

12.3 A Finnish soldier guards a pile of frozen corpses of Red Army soldiers in the Petsamo region of northern Finland in February 1940. The body on the extreme left froze to death in a squatting position.

12.4 'Rendez-vous'.

Source

Cartoon: 'Rendez-vous' by David Low. Published in the *Evening Standard,* September 1939. Copyright the David Low Trustees and the *Evening Standard.*

This cartoon appeared in a British newspaper in September 1939. Study it and answer the questions below.

(1) Identify the two men who are greeting each other.
(2) Which country is represented by the dead body, and what had the two men done to that country in the weeks before the cartoon was published?
(3) The two men are greeting each other with a smile but the words they are speaking reveal their true feelings. When was the temporary friendship between them formed and when and why did it come to an end?
(4) The country represented by the dead body was not the only country under threat because of the agreement between the two men. Name the other countries which were threatened by their agreement and specify which of them were conquered in the period 1939–40 and by whom.

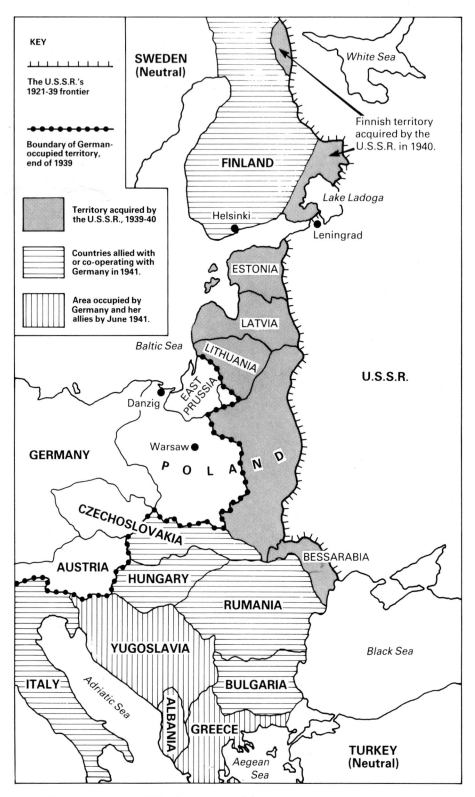

KEY

┼┼┼┼┼┼┼┼┼┼┼
The U.S.S.R.'s
1921-39 frontier

●━●━●━●━●━●━●
Boundary of German-
occupied territory,
end of 1939

Territory acquired by
the U.S.S.R., 1939-40

Countries allied with
or co-operating with
Germany in 1941.

Area occupied by
Germany and her
allies by June 1941.

SWEDEN
(Neutral)

White Sea

FINLAND

Finnish territory
acquired by the
U.S.S.R. in 1940.

Lake Ladoga

Helsinki

Leningrad

ESTONIA

LATVIA

Baltic Sea

LITHUANIA

U.S.S.R.

EAST
PRUSSIA

Danzig

GERMANY

Warsaw

P O L A N D

CZECHOSLOVAKIA

BESSARABIA

AUSTRIA

HUNGARY

RUMANIA

Black Sea

YUGOSLAVIA

ITALY

Adriatic Sea

BULGARIA

ALBANIA

GREECE

Aegean
Sea

TURKEY
(Neutral)

12.5 Central Europe 1939–41

Two versions of the Winter War

Here are two passages from history textbooks. Both describe the Winter War of 1939–40. One is from a Soviet textbook and the other from a British textbook. The books were written for students of similar ages. See if you can tell which is which. What clues are there in each passage to the nationality of its author? The answer is at the end of the chapter.

Passage A
'The Soviets decided that they would like to move the Finnish frontier further away from Leningrad and offered the Finns some Soviet territory in return. The Finns made some concessions but would not agree to Soviet naval bases on their soil, so the Soviet Union . . . attacked Finland on 30th November 1939. The Winter War cost the Red Army some 175 000–200 000 dead and 200 000–300 000 wounded and the Finns 23 000 dead. The longer the war continued the more likely France and Great Britain were to intervene so a lenient peace was concluded on the 12th March 1940. The war revealed the incompetence of the Red Army and Stalin moved quickly to remedy the situation.'

Passage B
'At that time the Soviet-Finnish border passed 32 kilometres from Leningrad . . . . The Finnish government declined the invitation of the U.S.S.R. to conclude a mutual aid agreement and broke off negotiations concerning the exchange of territory near Leningrad for twice as much territory in Karelia. . . . Thus Finnish reactionary forces, incited by Fascist Germany and the other imperialist powers, unleashed war against the Soviet Union . . . . The Red Army offensive on the Karelian isthmus began on 11th February 1940. Over a period of twenty days fierce battles took place, the 'Mannerheim Line'* was breached and the armed forces of Finland defeated. Having suffered defeat, the Finnish militarists sued for peace.'

* The Finnish defences.

The U.S.S.R. and Japan

When the Japanese invaded Manchuria in 1931 Stalin re-established relations with the Kuomintang. Japan's expansionist aims alarmed him, and from 1933 he was worried that Russia might have to fight a war on two fronts against Nazi Germany and Japan. Knowing that the Russians could not win such a war, he hoped that the Japanese would get bogged down in a long war in China. The signing of the Anti-Comintern Pact by Germany and Japan in 1936 deepened his fear of war on two fronts. The Pact, which Italy signed a year later, was a general agreement to oppose the spread of Communism.

In 1937 full-scale war broke out between China and Japan. Stalin ordered the Chinese Communists to co-operate with the Kuomintang against the Japanese and began once more to supply the Chinese with arms and military advice. In 1938–9 Japanese troops invaded the Nomonhan region of Outer Mongolia, then under Russian control. Russian troops commanded by General Georgi Zhukov decisively defeated the Japanese in fierce fighting in the area of Khalkin Gol. This brief war gave the Red Army valuable battle experience and deterred the Japanese from making any further attacks on Russian territory. In April 1941 Russia and Japan signed a Neutrality Pact. Stalin had avoided war on two fronts.

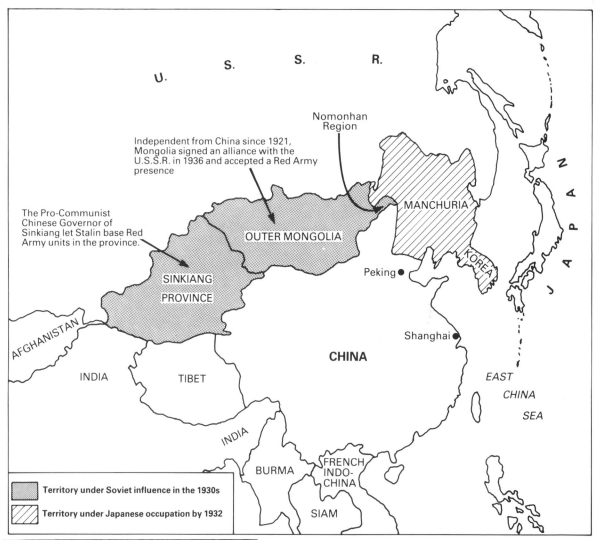

12.6 The U.S.S.R. and the Far East in the 1930s.

Sources
Passage A is from *The Soviet Union since 1917* by Martin McCauley, Longmans, London, 1981, pp. 100–1.
Passage B is from *The Russian version of the Second World War.* Sub-titled *The History of the War as taught to Soviet children.* Translated by Marjorie Vanston and edited by Graham Lyons. Published by Facts on File, New York, 1983. UK rights retained by the editor at 19 Battledean Road, London N.5.

13 The U.S.S.R. in the Second World War

'Operation Barbarossa'

In the early hours of the morning of Sunday, June 22nd 1941, German forces launched a large-scale offensive against the U.S.S.R. The Russians were taken by surprise. The morale of the Red Army was low and many of its ablest officers had been killed in the Purges. By late 1941 the Germans had advanced to within a few miles of Moscow. Their advance was halted as much by the severity of the winter weather, for which they were ill-prepared, as by Russian resistance. Winter gave the Russians a much needed breathing space and transformed what had been a blitzkrieg (lightning war) into a war of attrition.

The brutality of the Germans to the Russian civilian population and to Russian prisoners of war, over three million of whom were to die of disease and hunger, united the Russian people behind their leaders. Even those who disagreed with the Communist system supported Stalin's government in the national emergency. Stalin encouraged this support by urging people to fight and work not out of loyalty to Communism but out of loyalty to Mother Russia. He won the support of the Church by lifting many of the restrictions that had been imposed on it.

The Russian people had suffered terrible hardships since 1917 and were able to endure conditions that might have broken the will of a people used to a higher standard of living. The government resorted to 'Iron Discipline' once more. Holidays were abolished and the penalties for absenteeism were made more harsh. Political Commissars accompanied the troops to the front, and the death penalty was imposed not only in cases of desertion but also when troops failed to attack with sufficient vigour.

Much of Russia's agricultural and industrial capacity was in the areas overrun by the Germans in 1941. During the early months of the war, the Russians dismantled 1 500 factories and moved them by train, together with their machinery and workforces, to the area east of the Urals, where they would be out of range of German bombers. Machinery, raw materials and food that could not be moved were destroyed in a thorough 'scorched earth' policy.

The turning-point of the war

The turning-point of the war came in the years 1942–3. In 1942 the Germans launched an offensive which took them as far as the Caucasus Mountains. The advance was halted by the Russians at the city of Stalingrad on the Volga. There was desperate house-to-house fighting in the city in the autumn of 1942 as workers and Red Army soldiers defended houses, factories and grain silos. In November the Red Army counter-attacked and soon a quarter of a million men of the German Sixth Army were trapped in the Stalingrad area. In late January and early February 1943 they surrendered. The battle of Stalingrad was the Red Army's first positive victory of the war.

During 1943 the Russians built up their tank strength, thanks in part to help from Britain and the U.S.A. Nearly 17 000 000 tons of supplies were shipped to Russia by Britain and America between 1941 and 1945. About a quarter of this came by the Arctic convoy route to the port of

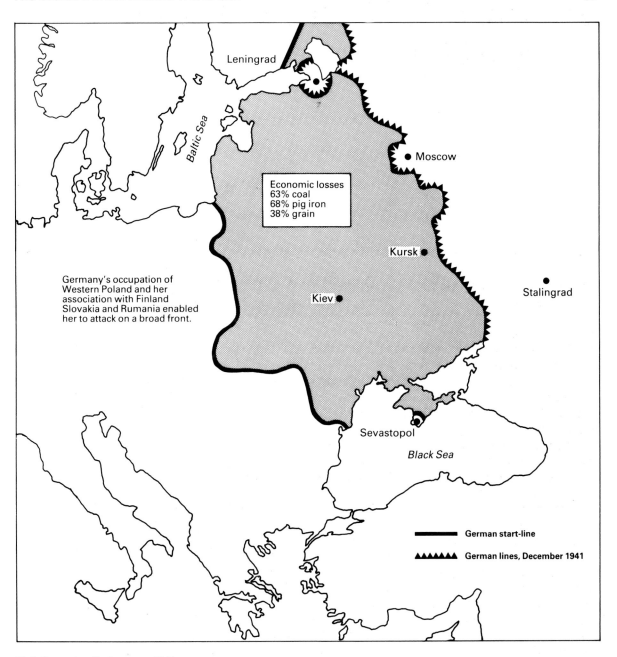

13.1 Operation Barbarosa – 1941.

Archangel and the goods were delivered despite terrible losses.

When the Germans launched an offensive in July 1943 with the intention of recapturing the city of Kursk, the Russians were able to counter-attack in force. Under the command of General, later Marshal, Zhukov the Red Army won the greatest tank battle of the war and then went onto the offensive. The Germans had lost the initiative and though they scored further victories, the tide of the war had turned against them.

13.2 Red Army soldiers fighting in the ruins of Stalingrad.

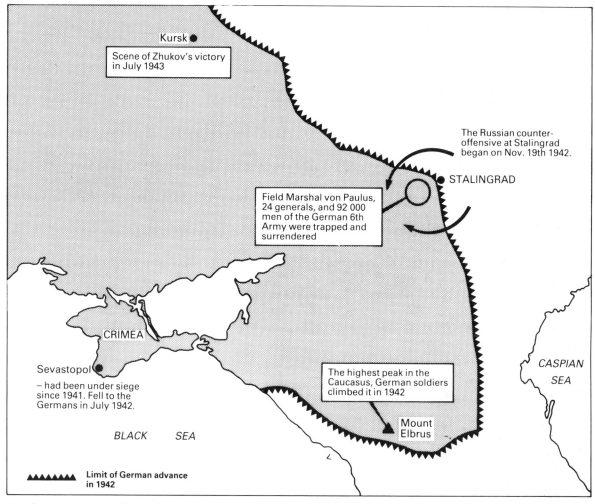

Kursk ●

Scene of Zhukov's victory
in July 1943

The Russian counter-
offensive at Stalingrad
began on Nov. 19th 1942.

● STALINGRAD

Field Marshal von Paulus,
24 generals, and 92 000
men of the German 6th
Army were trapped and
surrendered

CRIMEA

Sevastopol ●

– had been under siege
since 1941. Fell to the
Germans in July 1942.

CASPIAN
SEA

The highest peak in the
Caucasus, German soldiers
climbed it in 1942

BLACK   SEA

Mount
Elbrus

▲▲▲▲▲▲▲▲   **Limit of German advance
in 1942**

13.3 Russian counter-offensive at Stalingrad.

13.4 A Soviet tank in action during World War II.

Partisans, prisoners and deportees

In the first few weeks of the war many of the non Great Russian inhabitants of the Western U.S.S.R. welcomed the Germans as liberators, especially in the Ukraine and Byelorussia. German atrocities soon put an end to this enthusiasm, and many civilians decided to fight back by joining the Partisans. The Partisans based themselves in the forests and marshlands of western Russia and conducted a guerrilla war against the Germans. Some of the worst German atrocities were committed in response to Partisan activities. The Jews in the German-occupied parts of Russia were rounded up and slaughtered. A hundred thousand of them died in a single massacre at Babi Yar near Kiev. Three million Russians were forced to work in Germany as slave labourers, and many of them died of hunger and overwork. When all these victims are added to the number of people killed in action the death toll of Soviet citizens in the Second World War comes to at least 20 000 000.

The atrocities were by no means all on the German side. Eight thousand Polish officers had been taken prisoner by the Russians in 1939, and none of them survived the war. The Germans claimed that many of them had been massacred by the Russians in the Katyn Forest near Smolensk, though the Russians assert that this atrocity was the work of the Germans. Between 1941 and 1944 eight of the nationalities who lived in the western parts of the U.S.S.R. were deported by Stalin's government to Siberia. In some cases, such as that of the Crimean Tatars, the reason was that Stalin could not trust peoples who had lived under German occupation. In other cases, such as the Kalmyks, Stalin simply wished to move a national minority out of western Russia and give their land to Great Russians. The deportations involved approximately 1.5 million people, over a third of whom died of hunger and disease. The death rate among the Crimean Tatars was 46%.

13.5 German troops prepare to execute young Soviet partisans in the western U.S.S.R. in 1941.

The Soviet advance on Berlin

In January 1944 the Red Army counter-attacked in the Leningrad area, ending the siege of the city by the Germans, which had begun in 1941 and lasted 879 days. A million Leningraders died during the siege, 632 000 of starvation and disease. By August 1944 Russian troops had advanced through Poland to within a few miles of Warsaw. In the south they had pushed the Germans back through Rumania and Bulgaria and by the end of the year they had freed much of Hungary as well.

The final Russian offensive of the war began in January 1945, and took the Russian army through western Poland and into Germany itself. In April the assault on Berlin began and, after heavy fighting, the city surrendered on May 2nd 1945. Hitler had committed suicide on April 30th.

The war against Japan

Until 1945 the U.S.S.R. played no part in the war against Japan, though Stalin promised his allies that he would attack the Japanese once the Germans had surrendered. He began his offensive in August 1945, just after the Americans had dropped the atom bomb on Hiroshima. In a brief but large-scale campaign the Red Army occupied Manchuria and Northern Korea. This was not an important contribution to the defeat of Japan, which was by then inevitable, but it did gain the Russians a considerable amount of territory and influence in the Far East.

13.6 The Siege of Leningrad, 1941–44 879 days.

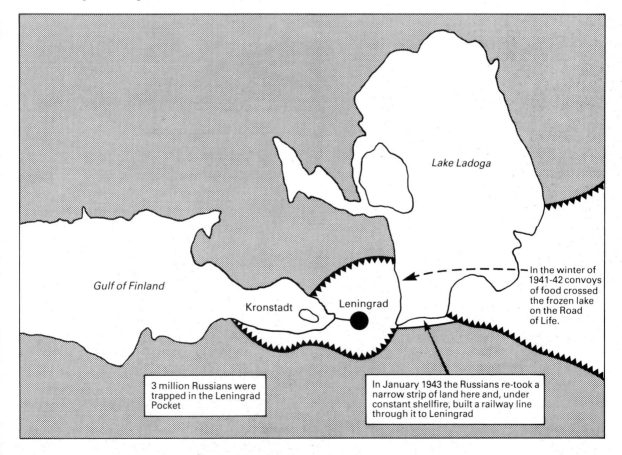

Lake Ladoga

Gulf of Finland

Kronstadt

Leningrad

In the winter of 1941-42 convoys of food crossed the frozen lake on the Road of Life.

3 million Russians were trapped in the Leningrad Pocket

In January 1943 the Russians re-took a narrow strip of land here and, under constant shellfire, built a railway line through it to Leningrad

13.7 Red Army soldiers hoist the Soviet flag on the ruins of the Reichstag building in Central·Berlin, 1945.

The U.S.S.R.'s relations with her allies

The war made Britain and the U.S.A. allies of the U.S.S.R., but the relationship was strained from the first. Stalin distrusted Churchill because he had been a vigorous advocate of British intervention in the Russian Civil War. Churchill and Roosevelt feared that a victorious Russia would dominate Eastern Europe, but they depended on the Russians to bear the brunt of the land war against Germany. Both the Russians and their allies feared that the other might try to make a separate peace with Hitler.

Stalin was very impatient at the delay in the opening of the Second Front in Europe. He first raised the possibility with the British in 1941, but was not satisfied by the Allied invasions of Sicily and Italy in 1943. The cartoon on page 103 reflects his impatience on this subject. Churchill and Roosevelt were not happy about Stalin's demand that after the war Russia should keep all the territory she had acquired in 1939–40, though towards the end of the war they realised that since the Red Army had occupied most of Eastern Europe they had little choice but to agree. In 1943 Stalin abolished Comintern in the hope of reassuring his allies that Russia's intentions were open and honest, but mistrust and suspicion grew during the last two years of the war.

13.8 'Under the Broomstick'.

Source
Cartoon 'Under the Broomstick', reproduced in Richards, Denis, *An Illustrated History of Modern Europe,* Longmans, 1977.

Study this cartoon, which was published in the U.S.S.R. in 1942, and answer the questions below. The words on the signpost are 'To the Soviet-German Front'. The strip of water which separates the man in the armchair from the man with the broomstick is labelled 'The Channel'.

Questions

(1) Who is the man in the armchair, and of which country was he Prime Minister in 1942?
(2) Who is the man with the broomstick? What is he doing?
(3) The cartoonist is suggesting that the country led by the man in the armchair has failed to keep a solemn promise in 1942 and has thus let the U.S.S.R. down. What was the promise? Had the country actually made such a promise? When did the country finally do what the cartoonist expected it to do in 1942?

The Teheran Conference

The first occasion on which Stalin, Churchill and Roosevelt met together was at the Teheran Conference in November 1943. Up to that point in the war the Russians had borne the brunt of the fighting on land, and this gave Stalin a moral authority over his allies, who were by no means confident of the success of their planned invasion of Northern France. Churchill suggested that the Russians should be allowed to keep the areas of Poland that they had seized in 1939, together with 'a port with access to broad waters' – a remark which Stalin interpreted as meaning a port in Northern Greece. This apparent generosity on the part of the British encouraged Stalin to take a much firmer line on Russia's other claims to territory in Eastern Europe. Stalin was determined that Eastern Europe should become a 'buffer zone' after the war, and that the Eastern European countries should have pro-Soviet governments. Only on the subject of Finland did Britain and America take a tough line at Teheran, and significantly Finland did not become a Russian-occupied satellite at the end of the war. At Teheran Stalin agreed that Russia would enter the war with Japan as soon as the Germans surrendered.

By the autumn of 1944 the question of who would control which parts of Europe after the war was becoming urgent. In October 1944 Churchill and Stalin met in Moscow and secretly agreed to divide Eastern Europe into spheres of influence. In Bulgaria, for example, Russia would have a 90% influence and Britain only a 10% influence. In Greece it would be the other way round. Roosevelt did not approve of these arrangements, which he saw as a cynical betrayal of the peoples of Eastern Europe.

13.9 (left to right) Stalin with Franklin D. Roosevelt and Winston Churchill at the Teheran Conference in 1943.

The Yalta Conference

In February 1945 the 'Big Three' met again at Yalta, in southern Russia. This Conference revealed that their aims were very different. Stalin was concerned with the security of the U.S.S.R. and believed that it depended on the Russians dominating Eastern Europe. He still saw the main threat to the U.S.S.R. as coming from Germany but was uncertain as to whether Germany should be divided into a number of smaller states or allowed to remain intact. Roosevelt saw the creation of the United Nations as the main guarantee of peace and security for all countries. He said that he did not expect to keep an appreciable number of American troops in Europe for more than two years after the Germans surrendered, an admission which encouraged Stalin to persist in his demands for Russian dominance in Eastern Europe. Churchill, who saw the U.S.S.R. as the main threat to the future security of Europe, was anxious to ensure a continuing American military commitment to Europe.

The Big Three discussed the future of Poland, and Roosevelt and Churchill agreed in principle that the Russians could keep the Polish territory they had conquered in 1939 and that the Poles would receive part of eastern Germany in compensation. Poland would be ruled at first by a coalition government including members of the Polish government-in-exile in London and the Polish Communists. Free elections would be held as soon as possible. Arrangements were made for the military administration of Germany which, together with its capital Berlin, was to be divided into British, French, American and Russian zones of occupation. Stalin reaffirmed his promise to declare war on Japan, and Roosevelt and Churchill agreed that the Russians could have Sakhalin and the Kurile Islands when peace was made with the Japanese. At this stage they thought that the war with Japan would be long and costly and that Russian help would be vital. A few months later, when the situation in the Far East had improved and the Americans had tested the first atom bomb, they regretted the concessions that they had made to Stalin.

At the end of the war Russia controlled a broad area of Europe stretching from the Baltic to the Adriatic. The Russians had won back much of the territory that they had lost as a result of the First World War, and now had the defensive 'buffer zone' in Eastern Europe that their rulers, Tsarist and Communist, had long desired. By August 1945 Russia had also avenged the defeat of 1905 at the hands of the Japanese. The Russian economy was in ruins, and America's possession of nuclear weapons left the U.S.S.R. at a strategic disadvantage, but the Soviet Union had played a vital role in the defeat of Nazism and had emerged as a World Power.

Facts and figures

Military casualties in the Second World War (total number of dead)

U.S.S.R.	7 500 000	
Germany	3 500 000	
Japan	1 500 000	(There are no reliable figures for
Great Britain	397 762	China. Estimates suggest over two
Poland	320 000	million Chinese soldiers were
Rumania	300 000	killed 1937–45.)
U.S.A.	292 000	
British Empire	117 749	

The War and the Soviet Economy

	1940	1945	1950
Industrial Output	100	92	173
Agricultural Output	100	60	99

(index number 100 = amount produced in 1940, the last full year of peace.)

Destroyed or seriously damaged during the war in the U.S.S.R.

Dwellings	6 000 000
Villages	70 000
Towns and cities	1 700
Factories	31 000
Collective Farms	98 000

Sources
Casualties: Gilbert, M. *Recent History Atlas,* Weidenfeld & Nicolson 1966, p. 93. Other statistics: Nove, A., *An Economic History of the U.S.S.R.,* Allen Lane 1969, Pelican ed. 1972, pp. 291, 287.

14 The origins of the Cold War

Russia had over eleven million men under arms in 1945 but demobilised rapidly, so that by 1948 the Red Army numbered 2 874 000, fewer than in 1941. This demobilisation happened despite the fact that Stalin was deeply suspicious of the Western Powers (the U.S.A., Britain and France). He resented the abrupt way in which President Truman had cut off Lend-Lease aid after Germany's surrender, and was angered by the Americans' refusal to grant economic aid to the war-torn U.S.S.R. The fact that Russia had suffered the heaviest losses of all the victor powers encouraged Stalin to believe that he was entitled to territorial gains in Eastern Europe, and the various promises that Churchill and Roosevelt had made in the period 1943–5 (see Chapter 13) strengthened that belief. Stalin believed, incorrectly, that Truman wanted to maintain a large U.S. military presence in Europe. He remembered the Civil War and feared that the Western Powers might take advantage of the U.S.S.R.'s weakness to attack her. The British and Americans were alarmed by Stalin's territorial ambitions and, mindful of how the policy of Appeasement in the 1930s had encouraged Hitler's aggression, they were determined not to make the same mistake with Stalin. This mutual distrust and uncertainty soon developed into a confrontation between the two sides which became known as the 'Cold War' – 'Cold' because, at least in Europe, the conflict stopped short of actual fighting.

The Potsdam Conference

The death of Roosevelt in April 1945 and the defeat of Churchill and the Conservatives in the British General Election of July 1945 meant that Stalin was the only member of the wartime 'Big Three' still in power by the end of the Potsdam Conference, which happened in July 1945. At the Conference U.S. President Harry S. Truman and British Prime Minister Clement Attlee confirmed the arrangements made at Yalta (see Chapter 13), and agreed that Germany should be treated as a single economic unit even though she was divided into four military zones. Stalin agreed that the Western Powers could have access to their zones of Berlin, which was deep inside the Russian zone of Germany, along transit routes for road, rail, air and canal traffic. Similar arrangements were made for Austria and her capital, Vienna. The long-term future of both countries would be decided at a future conference.

Since the Russians had suffered the most damage at the hands of the Germans, it was agreed at Potsdam that they should have the largest share of reparations. The bulk of Germany's industries were in the Western zones, so it was agreed that the Russians could have a quarter of the industrial plant confiscated from Western Germany as well as anything confiscated from the Russian zone. In return the Russians would send food, coal and raw materials from their zone to the Western zones to the value of 60% of the industrial plant that they received from the Western zones. These complex arrangements became a major source of disagreement between Russia and the Western Powers.

The future of Poland was also discussed at Potsdam. The U.S.S.R. had already, in April 1945, signed a treaty with the Poles fixing the western frontier of Poland along the line of the rivers Oder and Neisse and thus giving the Poles a slice of eastern Germany to compensate them for the loss of eastern Poland to Russia. Churchill and Roosevelt had agreed to this in principle, but Truman and Attlee were angry that the Russians had signed a treaty determining the future of a part of Germany without first officially consulting them. At Potsdam Stalin renewed his promise to hold free elections in all the countries occupied by the Red Army. He was determined to keep the Russian-occupied areas of Eastern Europe as a defensive 'buffer zone' so that if Russia was attacked from the West she would have greater defensive

14.1 (seated from left to right) Clement Attlee, Harry S. Truman and Stalin at the Potsdam Conference in 1945. Ernest Bevin (British Foreign Secretary) is standing second from the left, and Vyacheslav Molotov (Soviet Foreign Minister) is standing on the right, behind Stalin.

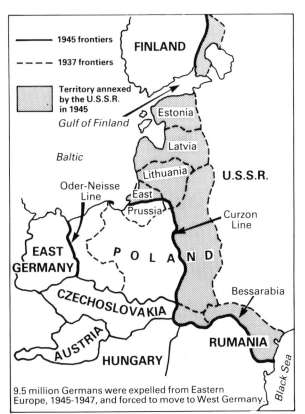

9.5 million Germans were expelled from Eastern Europe, 1945-1947, and forced to move to West Germany.

14.2 The U.S.S.R.'s territorial gains, 1945.

depth. He wanted the governments of the Eastern European countries to be friendly to the U.S.S.R. and to pursue foreign policies broadly in line with Russia's. As his mistrust of the Western Powers grew in the period 1945–7 he came to the conclusion that the only way to guarantee this was to make sure that the governments were Communist. It is unlikely that in 1945 he intended that the Russian zone of Germany should become a Communist state. Had this been his intention he would have been less keen to strengthen Poland at the expense of East Germany and to wreck the East German economy by stripping it of industrial plant.

Eastern Europe goes Communist

In Poland, Czechoslovakia, Hungary, Bulgaria and Rumania Communist governments were established within three years of the end of the war. The elections held in these countries in 1945–6 produced coalition governments in which Communists and non-Communists shared power. By 1948 the Communists had, by a mixture of political skill, threats and violence, worked their way into complete control of all these countries. They were helped by the divisions and disputes within and between the non-communist parties. The map of Eastern Europe gives more information about the Communist take-over in each of these countries.

In Albania and Yugoslavia Communist guerrillas had played an important part in driving out the Germans and Italians and Communist leaders Josip Broz Tito (Yugoslavia) and Enver Hoxha (Albania) were national heroes who needed little help from the Russians to establish themselves in power. Hoxha was happy to ally Albania with the U.S.S.R. since it was a poor country and needed aid. Tito, on the other hand, had no wish to see Yugoslavia become a Russian satellite. His refusal to obey Stalin's orders irritated the Russian leader and in 1948

Yugoslavia was expelled from Cominform (see below). Stalin unsuccessfully called on the Yugoslav Communists to overthrow Tito. Under Tito's leadership Yugoslavia developed close links with the West while remaining a Communist country.

Stalin was determined that the countries of Eastern Europe should be satellites of the U.S.S.R., in other words that they should have foreign and domestic policies approved by the Russians. In 1947 he established Cominform (The Communist Information Bureau) to ensure that the governments of Eastern Europe understood and obeyed his policies. At first Cominform's headquarters were in Belgrade but after Stalin's quarrel with Tito they were transferred to Bucharest in Rumania.

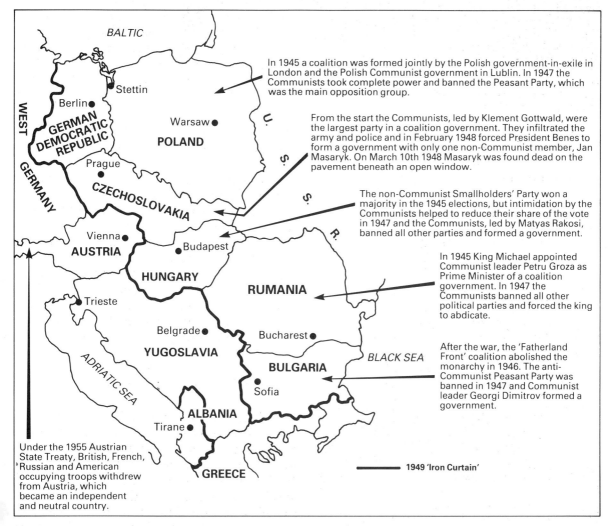

14.3 The 'Iron Curtain' countries 1945–49.

14.4 Tito addressing the Yugoslav People's Congress in October 1949. In this speech he accused COMINFORM of trying, on Stalin's orders, to stir up civil war in Yugoslavia.

Cominform continued to function until it was abolished in 1956.

In 1949 Stalin set up the Council for Mutual Economic Assistance (also known as COMECON or C.M.E.A.) to co-ordinate the economic policies of the satellite states and the U.S.S.R. COMECON forced the satellite states to produce what Russia needed and to sell to the Russians at artificially low prices. Stalin expected complete obedience from the Communist Parties in the satellite states, and purged those of their leaders who were suspected of 'Titoism' – by which he meant questioning the authority of the U.S.S.R. Leading Communists such as Gomulka (Poland) and Kadar (Hungary) were imprisoned for Titoism, while others such as Slansky (Czechoslovakia) were executed.

Greece, Turkey and Iran

At Potsdam Stalin demanded that Russia should be given the Greek port of Alexandroupolis as a naval base, reminding the Western Powers of Churchill's suggestion (at the Teheran Conference) that Russia should be given a deep water port. The demand was refused. In Greece, which according to the Moscow Agreement of 1944 (see Chapter 13) was largely under British influence, a civil war had broken out between Communists and anti-Communists. The British believed that Stalin was encouraging and financing the Greek Communists, though when it became clear that Britain and the U.S.A. were determined to prevent a Communist victory in Greece Stalin was careful to distance himself from the conflict and to say nothing in support of the Greek Communists.

In 1945–6 Stalin demanded the return of the provinces of Kars, Artvin and Ardahan which the Turks had gained from the Russians at the end of the First World War. The Turks appealed to the Western Powers for help, and Britain and the U.S.A. sent financial aid and a naval task force to Turkey to make it clear that they would not tolerate Russian aggression. In the face of this determination, Stalin dropped his demands.

During the war both Britain and Russia had stationed troops in Iran. The British kept their promise to withdraw their forces within six months of the end of the war, but the Russian troops stayed on and were only withdrawn after protests from the Iranian government. Even then Russian soldiers remained in the Iranian province of Azerbaijan to support pro-Communist Tudeh guerrillas in their fight for independence. Firm pressure from Britain and the U.S.A. was all that was needed to persuade Stalin to withdraw from Iranian Azerbaijan. The speed with which he backed down over Greece, Turkey and Iran suggests that he was 'trying it on' – probing to see how far he could go without upsetting the Western Powers. Britain and the U.S.A. regarded these crises, together with the emergence of Communist governments in Eastern Europe, as evidence that Russia was aggressive and a threat to Western Europe. Winston Churchill expressed this view in a famous speech delivered at Fulton, Missouri in March 1946. An extract from it is printed on page 111. The speech puzzled Stalin, who regarded Eastern Europe as part of his legitimate sphere of influence. He pointed out that he had not interfered with countries, such as Belgium, within the Western Powers' sphere of influence. The Fulton speech seemed to confirm his view that Britain and the U.S.A. were ganging up on the U.S.S.R.

Winston Churchill's speech at Fulton, Missouri, March 16th 1946

Read this extract carefully and then answer the questions below.

'A shadow has fallen upon the scenes so lately lighted by the allied victory. Nobody knows what Soviet Russia and its Communist international organisation intends to do in the immediate future or what are the limits, if any, to their expansive and proselytising tendencies. I have a strong admiration and regard for the valiant Russian people and for my wartime comrade, Marshal Stalin. There is sympathy and goodwill in Britain . . . we understand the Russian need to be secure on her Western frontier from all renewal of German aggression. We welcome her to her rightful place among the leading nations of the world. . . . It is my duty, however, to place before you certain facts about the present position in Europe.

From Stettin on the Baltic to Trieste on the Adriatic an iron curtain has descended across the Continent. Behind that line lie all the capitals of the ancient states of Central and Eastern Europe – Warsaw, Berlin, Prague, Vienna, Budapest, Belgrade, Bucharest and Sofia. All these famous cities and the populations around them lie in the Soviet Sphere, and all are subject in one form or another not only to Soviet influence but to a very high and increasing measure of control from Moscow. Athens alone, with its immortal glories, is free to decide its future at an election under British, American and French observation. The Russian-dominated Polish Government have been encouraged to make enormous and wrongful inroads upon Germany, and mass expulsions of millions of Germans on a scale grievous and undreamed of are now taking place. The Communist Parties, which were very small in all these Eastern States of Europe, have been raised to pre-eminence and power far beyond their numbers and are seeking everywhere to obtain totalitarian control. Police governments are prevailing in nearly every case, and so far, except in Czechoslovakia, there is no true democracy. Turkey and Persia are both profoundly alarmed at the claims which are made upon them and at the pressure being exerted by the Moscow Government. . . .'

Source
Keesings Contemporary Archives – now owned by Longmans – 1946/8 volume, page 7770/A.

Questions

(1) Is Churchill technically correct in saying that the U.S.S.R. had a 'Communist international organisation' in March 1946?
(2) Why did Churchill say that the Iron Curtain ran from Stettin to Trieste, and why was this not the case by 1949?

(3) What did Churchill mean when he said that the Poles 'have been encouraged to make enormous and wrongful inroads upon Germany'? In what sense were they wrongful?
(4) What were the claims that Russia was making on Turkey and Persia (Iran) in 1946? Why were the Russians unsuccessful in pressing these claims?

The Truman Doctrine and Marshall Aid

Unable to cope with the civil war in Greece, the British appealed to the U.S.A. for help. Truman agreed to send financial aid to the anti-Communist government in Greece and in March 1947 he told the U.S. Congress that he was determined to assist any country that was in danger of turning Communist. This policy, which became known as the 'Truman Doctrine', meant that Russia would not be allowed to spread her influence beyond the territories she had occupied in 1945. Truman and Secretary of State George Marshall knew that the poverty and destruction caused by the war made the spread of Communism more likely, and they were especially worried by the strength of the French and Italian Communist Parties. In June 1947 Marshall announced the European Recovery Programme, or 'Marshall Plan', a scheme under which the U.S.A. would send money to Europe to finance the reconstruction of industry and agriculture. The sixteen countries who received Marshall Aid formed themselves into the Organisation for European Economic Co-operation (O.E.E.C.) in order to administer the 13 150 000 000 dollars of aid that the U.S.A. sent to Europe under the Marshall Plan. Marshall Aid was offered to the Russian-occupied countries of Eastern Europe, but Stalin and his foreign minister Molotov would not let them accept it, fearing that Russia's control over those countries would be diminished if they became dependent on American aid. Stalin saw the Marshall Plan as an attempt to create a bloc of prosperous, well-armed anti-Russian states in

Western Europe, and as further evidence of the Western Powers' aggressive intentions. This view is reflected in the extract from a Soviet newspaper printed on page 113.

The future of Germany

The Russians had no clear policy on the future of Germany and in the period 1945–6 concentrated on extracting reparations from that country. They forced almost ten million Germans from the area east of the Oder-Neisse line to flee to Western Germany, thus putting great pressure on food supplies in the West. In 1946 they stopped delivering food and raw materials from their zones to Western Germany, and the Western Powers responded by cutting off reparations deliveries to the Russian zone. The Potsdam agreement on reparations had broken down. At the beginning of 1947 the British and Americans merged their zones into a single economic unit called Bizonia. Later in the same year they proposed that Marshall Aid should be given to all four zones of Germany. When Stalin would not agree they sent Marshall Aid to their own zones, thus breaking the Potsdam agreement to treat the whole of Germany as a single economic unit.

In June 1948, as an important step towards rebuilding the economy of Western Germany, the Western Powers introduced a new currency, the Deutschmark. It was becoming clear that they intended to set up an independent state in Western Germany. Stalin was anxious to prevent this and responded by closing the road, rail and

---

A Soviet view of American foreign policy, 1947

This extract is from an article which appeared in 'Pionerskaya Pravda', a newspaper for young people in the U.S.S.R. It was first published in August 1947.

'President Truman has announced the following principles of American foreign policy: the United States will everywhere support with weapons and money reactionaries, Fascists who are hateful to their own people but who on the other hand are ready to place their country under American control. Two countries suitable for this were found at once: Greece and Turkey. Now they both have in fact come under American domination. Americans are building their military bases there, American capitalists are opening businesses and buying up all that seems to them profitable. For this the Greek and Turkish reactionaries, who are in power, are receiving from the Americans money and weapons for the struggle against their own people. But Greece and Turkey are too small, and American appetites are great. American expansionists are dreaming of all Europe, or at least Western Europe. Directly to propose that the European countries become American colonies such as Greece and Turkey is somewhat inconvenient. And so the "Marshall Plan" emerges in America. It was announced that the United States wanted "to help" the European countries to reconstruct their war-destroyed economies. Many believed this. But it was soon evident that the "Marshall Plan" was simply a cunning way of subjecting all Europe to American capital.'

Source
Smith, Walter Bedell, *'Moscow Mission 1946–9'*, W. Heinemann, London, 1950, pp. 165–6.

(1) How accurate is the version of the 'Truman Doctrine' given in the first sentence of the extract?
(2) Why did the Americans become involved in the internal affairs of Greece and Turkey, and with what results?
(3) Why was Stalin anxious to persuade the public in the U.S.S.R. and Eastern Europe that the Marshall Plan was 'a cunning way of subjecting all Europe to American capital'?
    What private reasons did Stalin have for objecting to the Marshall Plan?

canal links between Western Germany and West Berlin. It was impossible to close the air corridors without shooting down Western aeroplanes, which would have been an act of war, but Russian fighters 'buzzed' Western aircraft using the corridors. Stalin hoped that the blockade of West Berlin would force the Western Powers to abandon their zones in the city and that it would prevent or delay the setting up of a West German state. Truman commented: 'We are going to stay. Period!' From June 24th 1948 to May 9th 1949, when Stalin lifted the blockade, the Western Powers kept the two million West Berliners supplied by a continuous airlift. At the height of the operation British, French and American planes were bringing in 13 000 tons of supplies a day, and planes were arriving and departing from West Berlin's three airfields at the rate of one every thirty seconds.

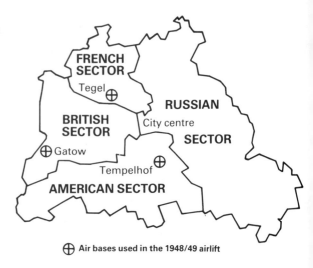

⊕ Air bases used in the 1948/49 airlift

14.5 Sector boundaries in Berlin since 1945.

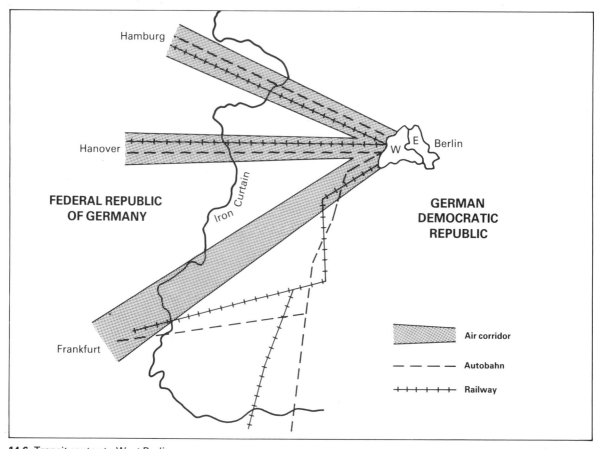

14.6 Transit routes to West Berlin.

14.7 During the Berlin Airlift of 1948–9 Allied flying-boats made use of West Berlin's extensive lakes. The 50 ton Sunderland flying-boat in the picture has just unloaded its cargo onto the barge in the foreground.

In the aftermath of the Berlin Blockade, elections were held in Western Germany and on September 1st 1949 the Federal Republic of Germany came into existence. On October 7th 1949 the German Democratic Republic was established in the Russian zone. The Russian Sector of Berlin became its capital. Both sides took these steps without consulting the other. The Russians and the Western Powers continued to station troops on German soil, and the Communist government of East Germany was from the start strongly loyal to the U.S.S.R.

NATO

By 1948 Truman had come to the conclusion that it would be necessary to keep large numbers of American troops in Western Europe to counteract what he saw as a Russian threat. In April 1949 the U.S.A. joined with eleven other nations to establish the North Atlantic Treaty Organisation (NATO). Its purpose was defensive, but from the start the Russians viewed it as a threat. In September 1949 it became apparent that the U.S.S.R. had successfully tested an atom bomb. Truman was alarmed by this and gave way to pressure from his own armed services to increase military expenditure and to develop the Hydrogen Bomb.

The U.S.S.R. and the United Nations

Roosevelt had hoped for a world organisation more effective than the League of Nations and strong enough to guarantee collective security. Stalin was more cynical. He realised that the United Nations would be little more than a facade disguising the conflict between the superpowers, Russia and America. He knew that the U.S.S.R. would be outvoted in the U.N. by America and her allies and his main concern was to secure a constitution for the U.N. which would compensate for Russia's weakness. At the Dumbarton Oaks Conference (1944) and at Yalta he insisted that the Security Council of the U.N. should only be able to take action with the unanimous agreement of its members. This would mean that the U.S.S.R. would have an effective veto. He also demanded that the republics which made up the U.S.S.R. should be individually represented at the U.N., though eventually he agreed to an arrangement whereby only the Ukraine and Byelorussia would have separate representation, so that the U.S.S.R. would have three seats in the General Assembly. On the issue of the Security Council veto Stalin got his way.

The Cold War spreads

During the period 1945–54 it became clear that Britain and France were no longer militarily or economically able to maintain their large overseas empires. The break-up of these empires might destabilise many areas of the world, and this prospect alarmed the Americans, who believed that such destabilisation would assist the spread of Communism. The Americans began to adopt the role of 'World Policeman' which the British and the French were abandoning.

After the defeat of the Japanese in 1945, Civil War broke out in China between the Communists and the Kuomintang. Stalin did not believe that the Communists, under Mao Tse-tung (Mao Zedong) had much chance of winning, and he continued to negotiate with the Kuomintang government of Chiang Kaishek until the Civil War ended in a Communist victory in 1949. This victory took Stalin by surprise. He quickly signed a Friendship Treaty with the new Communist government in February 1950, and began to send economic aid to China, though not on a generous scale. The prospect of a strong and united China worried him.

In Sinkiang and Manchuria the occupying Russian armies stayed on long enough after the end of the Second World War to loot the mineral resources of both areas. In North Korea they set up a pro-Russian Communist government headed by President Kim Il Sung, a Korean Communist who had trained and fought with the Red Army. In South Korea the Americans established a republic under President Syngman Rhee. Russian troops withdrew from North Korea in late 1948 and American troops from South Korea in 1949. The two Korean governments began to test each other's strength. Both hoped to unify Korea under their rule. The U.S.A. did not approve of Syngman Rhee's aggressive ambitions and in January 1950 Secretary of State Dean Acheson made it clear that the Americans did not regard South Korea as part of their 'defence perimeter' in the Far East. This was an open invitation to the North Koreans to attack, and in June 1950 they launched an invasion of South Korea.

The U.S.A. appealed to the U.N. Security Council. Between January and August 1950 the Russians were boycotting the U.N. because it had refused to recognise the Communist government of China, so the Russians were unable to veto the U.S. proposal that United Nations troops be sent to South Korea. Stalin thus found himself trapped into supporting the North Koreans in a war against United Nations forces. The prestige of Communism was at stake, so the war had to be continued until either victory or an acceptable compromise was achieved. Russian forces were not directly involved in the war, but without Russian aid and advice the Chinese and North Koreans could not have gone on fighting as long as they did.

In the early months of the war British, American and Commonwealth forces, fighting under the banner of the U.N., drove the North Korean invaders out of South Korea. By the end of 1950 they had carried the war into North Korean territory. The Chinese then intervened and forced the U.N. forces back. A military stalemate developed along the line of the 38th Parallel, which formed the boundary between North and South Korea. Truce negotiations began in July 1951 and an armistice was signed at Panmunjom in July 1953. By that time Stalin was dead. Though the war did not result in a Communist victory, the Russians benefited from it. China and North Korea became more dependent on Russian support and fear of the U.S.A. was to keep the Chinese reliant on the U.S.S.R. for several years after Stalin's death.

Stalin supported and encouraged Communist revolutionary movements in Malaya, Indonesia, the Philippines, Indo-China and India in the period 1945–53. A Communist regime under the leadership of Ho Chi Minh had been established in North Vietnam by 1954, but in other parts of Asia the Communists were defeated, notably by the British in the Malayan Emergency. This Communist activity in Asia further alarmed Britain and the U.S.A. The Americans were now convinced that if they did not 'hold the line' in Asia by defending the republic of South Vietnam then all the countries of South East Asia would fall to the Communists like a row of dominoes.

In 1954 they established the South-East Asia Treaty Organisation (SEATO) to contain the Communist threat.

It is difficult to apportion blame for the origins of the Cold War. Both sides broke promises and both sides developed an exaggerated fear of the other. The Western Powers sometimes asked for trouble by giving the Russians the impression that they did not care about certain areas. The probing and aggressive behaviour of the Russians helped to create the strong and permanent American military presence in Europe that the Russians feared so much. Stalin's successors inherited a dangerous international situation, and within a few months of his death the Russians tested their first Hydrogen Bomb.

15 Stalin's last years

The war strengthened Stalin's personal authority. The Supreme Soviet did not meet between 1939 and 1952, and Stalin governed the country with the help of a few trusted advisers. He continued to build up a cult of his own personality, encouraging citizens to regard him as a benevolent, all-wise father. Though he was at the height of his power, many of his actions in the period 1945–53 suggest that he felt insecure and that at the time of his death he was planning another great purge of the Party leadership.

Great Russian Nationalism

The War had aroused strong patriotic feelings in the U.S.S.R., and after 1945 Stalin tried to sustain them. He encouraged a narrow, Great Russian patriotism which emphasised not only the heroism of the Great Russians but also their cultural superiority. He wrote that once Communism had triumphed throughout the world, Russian would be the only language spoken on the planet. He encouraged historians

15.1 Stalin in later life.

Eyewitness

Milovan Djilas, a Yugoslav Communist, met Stalin and other Russian leaders on several occasions in the 1940s. He later became very disillusioned with Stalin's type of Communism. In his book 'Conversations with Stalin' he described those meetings.

'He (Stalin) was of a very small stature and ungainly build. His torso was short and narrow, while his legs and arms were too long. His left arm and shoulder seemed rather stiff. He had quite a large paunch, and his hair was sparse, though his scalp was not completely bald. His face was white, with ruddy cheeks.... His teeth were black and irregular, turned inwards. Not even his moustache was thick or firm. Still, the head was not a bad one; it had something of the common people, the peasants, the father of a great family about it — with those yellow eyes and a mixture of sternness and mischief.'

Stalin tells a joke

'One of our men was leading a group of German prisoners, and on the way he killed them all but one. They asked him, when he arrived at his destination: "And where are all the others?". "I was just carrying out the orders of the Commander in Chief", he said, "to kill every one to the last man — and here is the last man." '

Source
Djilas, M. *Conversations with Stalin,* tr. M. B. Petrovich, Pelican Books, 1969, pp. 52, 66.

---

to attribute every important discovery to Great Russians, and schoolchildren in the U.S.S.R. are still taught that the steam engine was invented not by James Watt but by Ivan Polzunov. The irony of Stalin's emphasis on Great Russian patriotism was that he himself was not a Great Russian, but a Georgian.

Industrial Recovery

The economy of the U.S.S.R. was in ruins at the end of the war, and 31 000 factories had been wrecked in the fighting. In 1946 Stalin announced a fourth Five Year Plan whose aim was the rapid reconstruction of industry. The Plan was financed by increasing the taxes paid by Collective Farmers and by keeping their standard of living well below that of the town-dwellers. Manchuria and the occupied areas of Eastern Europe were stripped of machinery, raw materials and skilled labour to assist the success of the Plan. Work began on major projects such as the Volga-Don Ship Canal and the hydro-electric power schemes at Kuibyshev and Stalingrad. The Plan achieved a considerable success. By 1950 many of the war-devastated regions of the U.S.S.R., such as the Ukraine, were producing as much as they had in 1940. In the production of coal, electricity, oil, steel and tractors the Plan's targets were beaten. By the time of Stalin's death a fifth Five Year Plan, which had been announced in 1952, was under way.

The Plan system with its targets and its severe penalties for managers who failed to meet them discouraged people from using their initiative and experimenting with new methods and products.

Agriculture

During the war the Collective Farmers had taken advantage of the chaotic conditions to enlarge their private plots and to take some of the Collectives' livestock into private ownership. In some areas of the U.S.S.R., Collective Farming broke down altogether. At the end of the war the government insisted on the return of all this land and livestock to the Collectives, and Collectivisation was reimposed on areas where it had broken down and imposed for the first time in the new Republics of the U.S.S.R., such as Estonia, Latvia and Lithuania. A serious drought in 1946 hampered recovery, and even by 1950 Russia's agricultural production had not quite returned to the pre-war level.

The 'Stalin Plan for the Transformation of Nature', announced in 1948, forced Collective Farm workers to waste time and money in an unsuccessful attempt to plant trees as windbreaks in the steppe regions of Russia. In general, agricultural planning was less sensible and effective than industrial planning. The peasants remained suspicious of the Communist Party. The high taxes and the low living standards that they had experienced were not likely to win them over to Communism. Nikita Khrushchev, a prominent Communist who had a great influence on agricultural policy during Stalin's last years, persuaded Stalin to join many of the Collective Farms together to form larger and more efficient units. In the period 1950–1 the number of Collective Farms was reduced from 250 000 to 95 000. This policy had a political as well as an economic purpose. The new Collectives were big enough to support Cells – the basic units of membership of the Communist Party. By 1952 75% of Collective Farms had a Communist Cell, whose members tried to explain Party theories to their fellow workers and win them over to Communism.

15.2 The rebuilding of the war damaged Dnieper Dam.

The birth rate

In the years after 1945 Stalin took steps to increase the birth rate. He was anxious to make up the losses of the war years and alarmed by the fact that the birth rate among Great Russians had slowed down while the other nationalities were breeding rapidly. The 1944 Family Law had made divorce more difficult and expensive to obtain. Women were given longer maternity leaves and mothers who over the years produced large numbers of babies were rewarded with medals and titles – 'Mother Heroine' if they produced ten or more infants.

Censorship and the Purges

Writers, artists and musicians had enjoyed a slightly greater degree of freedom under the unusual conditions of wartime. After 1945 Andrei Zhdanov, the Party's cultural watchdog, reimposed a strict censorship. Anyone whose work was intimate or personal in content, or western in style, was in danger of being criticised and condemned. The composers Shostakovich and Prokofiev and the poetess Anna Akhmatova were among those criticised by Zhdanov in this period.

15.3 Andrei Zhdanov, Communist Party chief in Leningrad and Stalin's cultural supremo.

The Purges had never ceased during the war and increased after it ended. Hundreds of thousands of Russians were still being shipped to labour camps in remote parts of the U.S.S.R. as alleged enemies of the state. The writer Alexander Solzhenitsyn, himself a victim of the Stalinist terror in the 1940s and 1950s, has likened the labour camps to an archipelago of grim islands – the *Gulag Archipelago*. 'Gulag' stands for Chief Administration of Collective Labour Camps. His novel *One Day in the life of Ivan Denisovich* tells what life in a labour camp was like.

The 'Leningrad Affair' and the Doctors' Plot

In 1948 Zhdanov, who had seemed the most likely successor to Stalin, died. Shortly after his death Stalin purged the Leningrad Communist Party, of which Zhdanov had been chief. Stalin disliked the way in which the Leningrad Communists ignored instructions from Moscow and pursued their own policies. The only important survivor of the 'Leningrad Affair' was Zhdanov's closest adviser, Alexei Kosygin.

In January 1953 Russian newspapers published a story which claimed that a group of doctors working in the Kremlin clinic had murdered Zhdanov and other leading Communists. Of the nine accused doctors, seven were Jewish. Stalin claimed that the 'Doctors' Plot' was a conspiracy organised by the British Secret Service. Persecution of the Jews in the U.S.S.R. grew worse, and several thousand people were arrested and interrogated. Stalin's colleagues, remembering the ruthless way in which he had acted in the 'Leningrad Affair', began to fear that he was planning another great Purge of the leadership, and that he would use the Doctors' Plot as evidence of a conspiracy within the Party. Then, on March 5th 1953, Stalin died of a stroke. Within a month it was publicly revealed that the Doctors' Plot was a fabrication.

Stalin – an assessment

In the years that followed his death Stalin was condemned by his successors and Russian history books were rewritten. The credit for his achievements was given to the Party and, if mentioned at all, he was criticised for being dictatorial and encouraging a cult of his personality.

Historians in the West are deeply divided in

their views of Stalin. Some argue that his policies, though morally indefensible, were politically necessary, and that they ensured that Russia was capable of defeating Germany. Others disagree, pointing to the chaos that rapid collectivisation caused and arguing that Russia could have achieved economic growth without Stalin's dictatorial methods. Some say that his rise to power was a tragedy for Russia because it turned her government into a dictatorship. Others blame the ruthless and centralised nature of Soviet government on Russia's isolation as the sole Communist country in a hostile world, or point out that Lenin was the real architect of the Soviet dictatorship and that Stalin was merely his disciple. For Communists Stalin is an historic embarrassment, and 'Stalinism' a dirty word. They argue that Communism need not necessarily lead to the kind of tyranny that Stalin practised. Some of Stalin's appalling cruelty must be attributed to the defects of his character rather than to the nature of Communism. The evidence suggests that he was a cruel, suspicious and at times irrational man. Nevertheless, a willingness to inflict misery on the present generation in order to secure better material conditions for future generations is a central part of Marxist-Leninism.

16 Khrushchev's Russia

Who will succeed Stalin?

After Stalin's death there was a power-struggle amongst the members of the Presidium, as the Politburo had been renamed in 1952, to determine who would be the new leader. At first Georgi Malenkov was appointed as Premier and General Secretary, but his colleagues quickly decided that this was too much power for one man and forced him to hand over the post of General Secretary to Nikita Khrushchev.

Malenkov, a highly-educated man from a middle class background, had spent most of his career in Moscow. He believed in government by experts rather than by enthusiastic but ignorant Party Members. Khrushchev was a crude and bumptious man from a peasant background. He had been the General Secretary of the Ukrainian Communist Party from 1938–49 before returning to Moscow to take charge of Russia's agricultural policy. In the course of the war he had formed close links with many senior army officers, including Marshal Zhukov.

All the members of the Presidium were wary of Lavrenti Beria, the head of the Secret Police (N.K.V.D.). Though he publicly supported Malenkov, Beria was widely believed to have ambitions to be Stalin's successor. His colleagues were determined to prevent this. Shortly

16.1 Georgi Malenkov on a visit to Carrington Power Station near Manchester in March 1956.

16.2 Lavrenti Beria, head of the N.K.V.D. from 1938–53.

after Stalin's death they announced that the 'Doctors' Plot' had been an invention and they blamed Beria for it. He was arrested in July 1953 and executed the following December.

The fall of Beria deprived Malenkov of one of his supporters. Malenkov was disliked by the Army Generals, who disapproved of his plans for reducing tensions between Russia and the West and cutting defence expenditure. Malenkov proposed to use the money saved on defence to improve the living standards of the Russian people. Khrushchev scornfully described this policy as 'Goulash Communism' and argued that defence expenditure should be increased. He and Malenkov also disagreed about agriculture. Malenkov favoured an 'industrial' approach – building up the engineering and chemical industries of the U.S.S.R. in order to provide farm machinery and fertilisers. Khrushchev argued that these methods were too slow. He suggested that large areas of unused or 'virgin' land should be brought under cultivation using a large labour force and simple methods. The Presidium adopted his plan, and Komsomol volunteers and army conscripts were sent to Siberia, Kazakhstan and the Volga region to bring the new land under cultivation. By 1956 35.9 million hectares of virgin land had been put to use – an area equivalent to all the cultivated land in Canada. Harvests were good in the early years, and the success of the scheme strengthened Khrushchev's position in the Presidium.

By February 1955 Khrushchev had enough allies in the Presidium to outvote Malenkov and force him to resign the premiership. Nikolai Bulganin became premier, and Marshal Zhukov succeeded Bulganin as Defence Minister. Malenkov remained a member of the Presidium and was given the post of Minister for Electric Power Stations.

Khrushchev changes sides

Having defeated Malenkov, Khrushchev proceeded to adopt most of his ideas. He announced his intention of raising living standards and working for peaceful co-existence with the West. Since these policies were radically different from those pursued by Stalin, Khrushchev felt that it

16.3 Nikita Khrushchev. This photograph was taken during an official visit to France. Khrushchev travelled abroad far more often than Stalin.

was necessary to undermine Stalin's reputation in order to put the policies into practice.

The Secret Speech

During the Twentieth Congress of the Communist Party of the Soviet Union in February 1956, Khrushchev made a long speech in which he condemned Stalin for being a dictator, for encouraging a cult of his own personality and for mishandling the development of Russian agriculture. He also read out Lenin's Political Testament (see Chapter 9). The speech, which became known as the Secret Speech although Khrushchev intended that its contents should be circulated through the Party, stunned Communists in the U.S.S.R. and elsewhere. They had been taught to revere Stalin as a wise, benevolent and successful leader and they were bewildered to learn part of the truth about him. An extract from the speech is printed on page 125.

Khrushchev's 'Secret Speech'

Study this extract from the lengthy speech that Khrushchev made to the 20th Congress of the Soviet Communist Party and then answer the questions below.

'After Stalin's death the central committee began to implement a policy of explaining concisely and consistently that it is impermissible and foreign to the spirit of Marxist-Leninism to elevate one person, to transform him into a superman with supernatural characteristics akin to those of a god. Such a man supposedly knows everything, and is infallible in his behaviour. Such a belief about a man, and specifically about Stalin, was cultivated among us for many years. . . . We have to consider this matter seriously and analyse it correctly in order to preclude any possibility of a repetition in any form whatsoever of what took place during Stalin's life. He did not tolerate collective leadership or work and practised bestial violence not only towards everything which opposed him but also towards anything which his capricious and despotic character found to be against his concepts.

Stalin acted not through persuasion, explanation and patient co-operation with people, but by imposing his views and demanding absolute submission. Whoever opposed this concept or tried to prove his own viewpoint and the correctness of his position, was doomed to be removed from the leading collective and to suffer subsequent moral and political annihilation . . . Stalin originated the concept of "enemy of the people". This term automatically rendered it unnecessary that the ideological errors of a man or men engaged in controversy be proved: this term made possible the usage of a most cruel repression . . . against those who were only suspected of hostile intent, or against those who had bad reputations. . . . Stalin discarded Lenin's methods of convincing and educating: he abandoned the method of ideological struggle for that of administrative violence, mass repression and terror. He acted on an increasingly large scale and more stubbornly through punitive organs, often violating all existing norms of morality and Soviet law.'

Questions

(1) Why is it 'impermissible and foreign to the spirit of Marxist-Leninism' to develop a cult of a leader's personality? If you are unsure of the answer, look again at the section on Marxism in Chapter 2 and at the final paragraph of Chapter 8.

(2) Give an example of someone who 'was doomed to be removed from the leading collective' because his views did not coincide with Stalin's. What was that person's ultimate fate?

(3) Is the portrait of Lenin as a patient, tolerant man who was prepared to educate political opponents instead of destroying them entirely true? Refresh your memory by looking again at Chapter 7.

Even before the Secret Speech, the Presidium had begun to relax Stalin's tyrannical system of government. The size and powers of the Secret Police had been reduced after the fall of Beria. Many political prisoners had been released, and the government had begun to rehabilitate some of the victims of the Stalinist purges, publicly declaring them innocent of the crimes for which they had gone to their deaths.

The 'Anti-Party Group'

Several of Khrushchev's Presidium colleagues disapproved of the Secret Speech and the de-Stalinisation of Russia. The troubles in Poland and Hungary (see Chapter 17) confirmed Molotov, Malenkov and Bulganin in their belief that Khrushchev's 'thaw' was a dangerous experiment. They were also alarmed by his plans to break up the large ministries in Moscow and decentralise government. In June 1957 they outvoted him in the Presidium and demanded his resignation. Khrushchev insisted that only the Central Committee could sack a General Secretary and his opponents unwisely agreed to put the matter to a vote of the Central Committee.

Khrushchev put his case to the Central Committee very cleverly. He labelled Molotov, Malenkov and Bulganin as 'the Anti-Party Group', portraying them as men who wished to keep power in the hands of civil servants in Moscow. Khrushchev's supporters made lengthy speeches in order to give the Red Army time to fly in more Khrushchevite members of the Central Committee from distant parts of the U.S.S.R. As General Secretary Khrushchev had been, since 1953, in a position to promote his own supporters onto the Central Committee and

he won the vote. Most of the Anti-Party Group lost their seats on the Presidium, but they were treated humanely. Molotov became ambassador to Outer Mongolia and Malenkov was sent to manage a Power Station in Kazakhstan. Bulganin resigned the premiership in 1958 and from then on Khrushchev held that office as well as the General Secretaryship.

The Thaw and the Arts

Though Khrushchev denounced Stalin's rigid censorship of the Arts, his own policy was only a little more liberal, and the troubles in Poland and Hungary in 1956 discouraged him from relaxing the censorship in the U.S.S.R. any further. He allowed the publication of books, such as Alexander Solzhenitsyn's *One Day in the Life of Ivan Denisovich*, which attacked the evils of Stalinism, but he criticised the poet and novelist Boris Pasternak, whose novel 'Dr. Zhivago' was published only in the West, for his 'bourgeois individualism'. Khrushchev himself was a simple minded man who knew what he liked and freely expressed his contempt for modern painting and music, dismissing one exhibition of modern art as 'rubbish' and 'dog shit'.

Khrushchev and the Churches

Khrushchev's attitude to religion was more repressive than Stalin's had been in the period 1941–53. Between 1960 and 1964 he reduced the number of functioning churches by two thirds, bulldozing many church buildings to the ground and forbidding the congregations to meet elsewhere. Most of the clergy accepted this persecution without public protests, arguing that the only way for the Church to survive was for its members to obey the law. Some Orthodox and Baptist clergy refused to obey, and the government responded by de-registering their churches and arresting all who attempted to use them.

Living standards and education

In 1953 the living standards of Soviet citizens were very low, but by 1964 they had improved considerably. Real wages increased and the government spent more money on welfare. Paid holidays, pensions, family allowances, better medical care and larger housing subsidies were among the benefits that Russians came to enjoy under Khrushchev's rule. As in Stalin's time, the Collective Farm workers were largely excluded from the welfare state, though the gap between their living standards and those of the urban workers narrowed in the period 1953–64. Fees for secondary and higher education were abolished. A seven hour working day became the norm and the harsh penalties for absenteeism were dropped. Workers were permitted to exchange jobs more freely and the minimum wage was raised. Technical and scientific education improved and the U.S.S.R. embarked on a programme of space exploration, achieving the first launch of an artificial earth satellite (Sputnik 1 in 1957) and the first manned spaceflight (by Yuri Gagarin in 1961).

Planning and Industry

In the years immediately after Stalin's death Malenkov was in charge of industry and Khrushchev ran agriculture. In 1953 Malenkov announced new targets to replace those of the Fifth Plan. The new targets emphasised consumer goods such as clothes, shoes, cycles and watches. The targets were very ambitious and were only achieved in a few areas of production, such as the manufacture of motor cycles.

A sixth Five Year Plan was announced in 1956, only to be replaced by a Seven Year Plan which ran from 1959–65. This Plan also

16.4 Yuri Gagarin, the Soviet cosmonaut who made the first manned space flight in 1961.

emphasised consumer goods, as well as calling for growth in the chemical industries to provide artificial fertilisers for agriculture.

In 1957 Khrushchev announced a great scheme of administrative reform. Many of the large and inefficient ministries in Moscow were closed down, and more than a hundred Regional Economic Councils (Sovnarkhozy) were set up to run the economy at a local level. This reform introduced another layer of muddle and inefficiency into Russia's already complex system of economic planning. By 1960 Khrushchev realised that the Sovnarkhoz system was not working. He tried to improve it by reducing the number of Sovnarkhozy and by appointing committees of officials to supervise their work. The result was that no one knew who was in charge or what was expected of them. Though some of the targets in the Seven Year Plan were achieved, rates of growth in industry remained low. Money had been diverted to finance armaments and space research, and other sectors of the economy lagged behind.

In October 1961, at the 22nd Party Congress, Khrushchev announced a new programme which would, he promised, achieve the goal of Communism within twenty years. By 1970 Russia would outstrip the U.S.A. in industrial output, and by 1980 the perfect society would be within sight. At the same Congress it was decided to remove Stalin's embalmed body from its place alongside Lenin in the Red Square mausoleum.

Agriculture

In 1953 agricultural productivity was low and the livestock population was too small. Khrushchev blamed this state of affairs on the high taxes that Collective Farm workers had to pay and on the low prices they received for their produce. He increased prices, cancelled the debts that many Collective Farms owed to the government, and cut taxes. The government began to invest more money in farm machinery and fertilisers and the ambitious Virgin Lands scheme described earlier in this chapter began. Many Collective Farms were transformed into State Farms. The Machine Tractor Stations were abolished and their equipment was sold to the Collective Farms. Repair Technical Stations were set up to provide a maintenance service for farm machinery. The early success of the Virgin Lands scheme encouraged Khrushchev to be ambitious, and the Seven Year Plan called for a 70% increase in agricultural output.

Output rose by only 14% during the Seven Year Plan, and yields from the Virgin Lands declined after 1958 because they had been farmed too intensively. The Collective Farms found it difficult to pay for the tractors that they

16.5 Khrushchev, a keen advocate of the planting of maize, admires the crop grown under the leadership of Hero of Socialist Labour Alexander Romanyuk at the Nove Zhytta Collective Farm.

purchased and there were not enough Repair Technical Stations. The prices of meat and dairy produce remained too low and livestock farming did not flourish as Khrushchev had hoped that it would. Khrushchev continually interfered in agricultural planning, forcing farmers to experiment with new crops and reforming the administration of agriculture. In 1963 he divided the Party's administration into two separate wings – one to control industry and the other to control agriculture. This reform worsened the confusion. Bad harvests in the early 1960s forced the government to raise food prices and this led to unrest in some towns and cities.

The fall of Khrushchev

Khrushchev attempted to divert his colleagues' attention from the failure of his economic and administrative reforms by pursuing an active foreign policy. His failures in that field, which are described in Chapter 17, helped to hasten his downfall. His colleagues objected to his boorish manners and to the fact that he promoted his relatives into important positions. They felt that he was beginning to develop a cult of his own personality. In October 1964 they united to oust him from power and to force him into retirement.

Facts and figures – The economy of the U.S.S.R. in the Khrushchev years

Agriculture

Grain harvest in millions of tons

1950	81.2	1954	85.6	1958	134.7
1951	78.7	1955	103.7	1959	119.5
1952	92.2	1956	125.0	1960	125.5
1953	82.5	1957	102.6	1965	121.1

Output of the Virgin Lands in millions of tons

1953	26.9
1955	27.7
1958	58.4

Population of the U.S.S.R. in millions (+ % living in towns and cities)

1951 181.6 40%
1956 197.9 45%
1961 216.3 50% – (the first time in history that there was as many Soviet citizens living in towns and cities as in the countryside.)

Questions

(1) Was agricultural output keeping pace with population growth? n.b. since harvests fluctuate with the weather it might be sensible to average out the figures for 1950, 51 and 52, for 1955, 56 and 57, and for 1958, 59 and 60 in order to make a

comparison with the size of the population in 1951, 1956 and
1961.

(2) Was agriculture becoming more efficient?– in other words were
the same number of people (or fewer people) managing to
grow more crops (n.b. obviously not everyone who lives in the
countryside actually works at growing food). For the purposes
of this calculation assume that 1/3rd of the rural population are
actually engaged in food producing.

Industrial output

	1955	1965
Electric Power (milliards of Kwh)	170.0	507.0
Crude Oil (millions of tons)	70.8	243.0
Coal (millions of tons)	390.0	578.0
Pig Iron (millions of tons)	33.3	66.2
Tractors (thousands)	163.0	355.0

Question

How do these rates of growth in industrial output compare with
those achieved under Stalin's leadership in the period 1928–40?
(see the tables on page 73).

Sources
Virgin Lands output: Nove, A. *An Economic History of the U.S.S.R.,*
Allen Lane, 1969, Pelican edition p. 334. Other statistics: Lewytzkyj,
B. *The Soviet Union: Facts – Figures – Data,* K. G. Saur, Munchen –
New York – London – Paris, 1979, pp. 174–191, 245–246, 280–81 and
287.

Khrushchev on the problems of administration

This extract is taken from Khrushchev's memoirs.

'Another reason for the failure of our agriculture to keep pace with the rest of our economy after the war was too much bureaucracy.... I don't for a minute deny the necessity of administration. I haven't forgotten Lenin's words: "socialism is management", but Lenin had it in mind that managers should serve socialism – not the other way round. When I was in the Ukraine both before and after the war, we were forever receiving from the ministry memos and directives that almost invariably ran counter to our understanding of what should be done. Sometimes the ministry's communications were a total waste of our time and energy, such as when the ministry sent us instructions on how to sow our sugar beet crop well after the seeds were already in the ground.... Every bulky administrative apparatus must somehow justify its existence. It does so by grinding out telegrams, dispatching inspectors every which way, quoting cable references back and forth ... and issuing proclamations which often come down to platitudes like "one should drink only boiled water".'

Questions

(1) What steps did Khrushchev take to free Russian agriculture and industry from bureaucratic muddle, and with what success?
(2) When Khrushchev writes 'another reason for the failure of our agriculture ...' he implies that bureaucracy was not the only problem from which Russian agriculture suffered. What other reasons were there for the poor performance of Russian agriculture in the period 1945–64?

Source
Khrushchev, N. S. *Khrushchev Remembers*, André Deutsch Ltd. 1971.

Timeline

The U.S.S.R. from Khrushchev to Chernenko

1953   Death of Stalin. Khrushchev becomes General Secretary, Malenkov becomes Premier.

1955   February: Malenkov forced to resign as Premier and succeeded by Bulganin.

1956   February: Khrushchev denounces Stalin in his 'Secret Speech' to the 20th Party Congress.

1957   June: Khrushchev defeats the Anti-Party Group.

1958   Bulganin resigns and Khrushchev becomes Premier.
Economic Policy, 1953–8.
1953 beginning of Khrushchev's 'Virgin Lands' scheme.
1956 Sixth Five Year Plan introduced, only to be dropped . . .
1958 . . . in favour of a Seven Year Plan, 1959–65.

1964   October: Khrushchev's colleagues remove him from office. He dies in 1977. Alexei Kosygin becomes Premier, Leonid Brezhnev becomes General Secretary.

1965   Beginning of the Kosygin Reforms (1965–70).

1966   The trial of Sinyavsky and Daniel signals the beginning of a government crack-down on Dissidents.
Beginning of the Eighth Five Year Plan (1966–70).

1971   The Ninth Five Year Plan begins.

1976   The Tenth Five Year Plan begins.

1977   Nikolai Podgorny resigns as President of the U.S.S.R. and is succeeded by Brezhnev.

1980   Resignation and death of Kosygin. Nikolai Tikhonov succeeds him as Premier.

1981   26th Party Congress. Targets announced for the 11th Five Year Plan to run from 1981–5.

1982   November: death of Leonid Brezhnev. Yuri Andropov succeeds him as General Secretary.

1984   February: death of Yuri Andropov. Konstantin Chernenko succeeds him as General Secretary.

17 Khrushchev's foreign policy

Peaceful Co-existence

In 1953 relations between the U.S.S.R. and the West were very tense. Khrushchev sought to reduce this tension by pursuing a policy of peaceful co-existence. This did not mean an end to the rivalry between Russia and the West. It meant that the rivalry would be pursued by any means short of outright war. The Western Powers thought, wrongly, that peaceful co-existence would mean that the Russians would stop interfering in the affairs of non-Communist countries. This misunderstanding as to the nature of peaceful co-existence made relations between Russia and the West more tense during Khrushchev's leadership. Khrushchev's personality did not help. His behaviour – he once removed one of his shoes and hammered it on the desk to emphasise the point that he was making in a speech to the United Nations – and his language, especially his famous remark 'We will bury you', alarmed Western leaders.

Pacts and encirclement

Behind Khrushchev's bluff, bullying exterior lay a real fear of the West. The Pacts which Presidents Truman and Eisenhower set up to contain the U.S.S.R. seemed menacing to the Russians and gave them the feeling of being encircled by an aggressive enemy. The language of Western leaders also alarmed the Russians. John Foster Dulles, U.S. Secretary of State in the 1950s, talked of the possibility of 'rolling back' the Russians from Eastern Europe, and contemplated adopting the Radford Plan, which called for 'massive retaliation' (the use of nuclear weapons) at the first sign of Russian aggression. This talk frightened the Russians into a determined effort to keep up with the U.S.A. in the nuclear arms race, though the backwardness of the Russian economy made this difficult.

Eastern Europe

Stalin's death and Khrushchev's condemnation of him created an expectation of change in the Communist states of Eastern Europe. In June 1953 Russian troops put down a workers' uprising in East Berlin. The rebels were protesting about the continuing presence of Russian troops in East Germany, the reparations policy, and poor working conditions. Russia immediately halted reparations deliveries, and agreed to pay the COMECON countries more for the goods that they sold to the U.S.S.R. Khrushchev permitted the release of some of those who had been imprisoned for 'Titoism' and re-established friendly relations with Yugoslavia, commenting that 'there is more than one road to socialism'.

The Warsaw Pact

In May 1955 the U.S.S.R. and the satellite states signed a twenty year defensive alliance and formed themselves into the Warsaw Pact. The Pact was set up as a counter-balance to NATO, of which West Germany became a member in 1955. It provided a reason for Russian troops to remain in the satellite states and enabled the U.S.S.R. to claim that the satellite states and the U.S.S.R. were equal members of a 'Socialist Commonwealth'.

Problems in Poland

The 'Thaw' in Russia created expectations of reform in Poland. Communism had not put down deep roots in Poland. Polish agriculture had not been collectivised. The Catholic Church remained very strong, and the deeply patriotic Poles resented the presence of Russian troops on their soil. In June 1956 workers in Poznan went

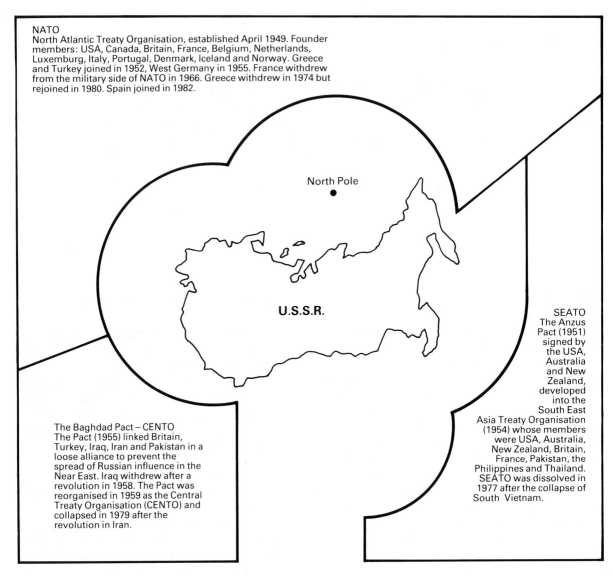

NATO
North Atlantic Treaty Organisation, established April 1949. Founder members: USA, Canada, Britain, France, Belgium, Netherlands, Luxemburg, Italy, Portugal, Denmark, Iceland and Norway. Greece and Turkey joined in 1952, West Germany in 1955. France withdrew from the military side of NATO in 1966. Greece withdrew in 1974 but rejoined in 1980. Spain joined in 1982.

North Pole

U.S.S.R.

SEATO
The Anzus Pact (1951) signed by the USA, Australia and New Zealand, developed into the South East Asia Treaty Organisation (1954) whose members were USA, Australia, New Zealand, Britain, France, Pakistan, the Philippines and Thailand. SEATO was dissolved in 1977 after the collapse of South Vietnam.

The Baghdad Pact – CENTO
The Pact (1955) linked Britain, Turkey, Iraq, Iran and Pakistan in a loose alliance to prevent the spread of Russian influence in the Near East. Iraq withdrew after a revolution in 1958. The Pact was reorganised in 1959 as the Central Treaty Organisation (CENTO) and collapsed in 1979 after the revolution in Iran.

17.1 Pacts and the containment of the U.S.S.R.

on strike in protest against working conditions. They demanded that Wladyslaw Gomulka, who had been expelled from the Communist Party for Titoism, be readmitted to the Party and to the government. The strike movement spread rapidly. Khrushchev put Russian troops in and around Poland on the alert, fearing that the Polish government might lose control of the situation. Then he flew to Warsaw to discuss the crisis with the leaders of the Polish Communist Party. He decided to allow Gomulka to emerge as the new leader of Poland and to purge some of the unpopular Stalinists in the government. Gomulka promised that Poland would remain a loyal member of the Warsaw Pact. Khrushchev calculated that using the Russian Army to crush the strike movement would have deepened the Poles' hatred of the Russians and would have created more problems than it solved.

The Warsaw Pact

Set up by the Warsaw Treaty, May 1955. Founder members: U.S.S.R., Poland, East Germany, Czechoslovakia, Hungary, Rumania, Bulgaria and Albania. In 1961 Albania sided with China in the Russo-Chinese quarrel and effectively ceased to be a member of the Pact, though she did not formally withdraw until 1968.

All Pact members have Russian troops stationed on their soil except Bulgaria and Rumania. Since 1972 the Rumanians have refused to join in Warsaw Pact military manoeuvres.

The Hungarian Uprising

In June 1956 the Russians permitted the Hungarians to dismiss their Stalinist leader Matyas Rakosi. His successor, Ernö Gerö, was unable to contain the Hungarian peoples' demands for greater freedom. In October 1956 street fighting broke out in the Hungarian capital Budapest between Hungarians eager for reform and Russian troops. In an attempt to defuse a dangerous situation the Russians agreed that Gerö should be replaced by a more liberal and more popular Communist, Imre Nagy. Nagy set up a new government which included two non-Communist members.

Public opinion was not satisfied with these changes, and there were demands for free elections and the withdrawal of Hungary from the Warsaw Pact. On November 1st the Nagy government decided to give in to these demands. The Russians responded by invading Hungary on November 4th. Red Army units crushed the Hungarians in bitter fighting which cost 7000 Russian and 30 000 Hungarian lives. Imre Nagy was imprisoned and later executed, and the Russians established a new government under the leadership of Janos Kadar, whom they regarded as more loyal to Moscow. Many Hungarians fled to the West. The Western Powers, though they applauded and encouraged the Hungarian Rising, felt unable to intervene. To do so would have meant risking a nuclear war, and the Western Powers were preoccupied with the Suez crisis.

Relations with Communist China

At first Khrushchev enjoyed good relations with the Chinese Communist government. He visited Peking in 1954 and gave the Chinese economic aid on a scale more generous than Stalin. These friendly relations did not last. Mao Tse-Tung (Mao Zedong) was shocked by 'de-Stalinisation'. He had revered Stalin, and accused Khrushchev of 'Revisionism' – departing from the true doctrines of Marxist-Leninism. Mao argued that the U.S.S.R. was no longer fit to lead the world Communist movement, and that China should take her place.

Mao regarded Khrushchev's policy of peaceful co-existence as the main evidence that Khrushchev had departed from the proper Communist line. Mao viewed the U.S.A. as the chief enemy of world Communism because of her intervention in Korea and her continuing support for the Chinese Nationalist Government on Taiwan. When the Chinese Communists bombarded the Nationalist-held islands of Quemoy and Matsu in 1958 Khrushchev refused to support them, because he was anxious not to antagonise the U.S.A. Khrushchev also disapproved of Mao's economic policies, refusing to support the 'Great Leap Forward'. In 1959 he decided not to fulfil his earlier promise to give the Chinese the money and the expertise that they needed to build nuclear weapons.

The World Communist Conference in Moscow in November 1960 failed to heal the breach between Russia and China, and by the

17.2 Budapest, October 1956. Hungarian students prepare to pull down a statue of Stalin.

end of 1960 the Russians had cut off all aid to China. A 'war of words' commenced between Moscow and Peking, and during the 1960s many of the Communist Parties throughout the world split into pro-Russian and pro-Chinese factions. In 1961 Albania broke off relations with the U.S.S.R. and sided with China. In 1962 there were clashes between Russian and Chinese soldiers along the disputed frontier of Sinkiang Province, and in the autumn of that year Russia gave diplomatic support to India in her border conflict with China.

The U.S.S.R. and the Third World

Stalin's policy of supporting Communist revolutions in Third World countries had met with little success and created fear and suspicion of the U.S.S.R. in the Third World. Many

Third World governments favoured a policy of non-alignment – maintaining friendly relations with both Russia and the Western Powers without becoming dependent on either. In practice non-alignment was impossible for many countries because they needed economic aid and the Russians and Americans were able to buy their support by granting aid with political and military strings attached. From 1960 onwards the Chinese were also seeking allies in the Third World by these means, though their economic backwardness meant that they could not compete on equal terms with the U.S.S.R. in this game of 'chequebook diplomacy'.

Khrushchev sought to win friends for the U.S.S.R. among the newly-independent nations of the southern hemisphere because he wished to extend Russia's influence and to 'leapfrog' over the system of British and American pacts which encircled the U.S.S.R. He hoped in time to weaken or to destroy those pacts and to win naval and military bases for the U.S.S.R. in strategically important areas such as the Mediterranean and the Indian Ocean.

India disliked the American-backed SEATO Pact, to which her rival Pakistan belonged, and needed foreign aid to develop her industry and agriculture. Under a Trade Agreement of 1955 the Russians undertook to build a steelworks at Bhilai in India, the first of many projects that they supported. Russia gave the Indians diplomatic support in their border disputes with China and Pakistan, and after the brief conflict with China in 1962 the Russians began to supply the Indian government with arms.

Gamal Abdel Nasser, the ruler of Egypt, was far from being a Communist, but he resented American interference in the Middle East and support for Israel. When Nasser nationalised the Suez Canal in 1956 he antagonised Britain and France, who owned the canal. Khrushchev supported the nationalisation and condemned Britain, France and Israel for their attacks on Egypt in November 1956. After the Suez crisis the Russians re-equipped the Egyptian armed forces and gave the Egyptians economic and technical aid. Russian engineers worked on the construction of the Aswan High Dam, and Khrushchev continued to support Nasser despite Nasser's frequent anti-Communist speeches.

The German Question

Khrushchev's attempt to achieve peaceful co-existence with the Western Powers began with a series of concessions. Russia abandoned her claims to Turkish territory and took the initiative in the talks that led to the Austrian State Treaty of 1955, under which all the Powers withdrew their troops from Austria and she became a neutral and independent country. In the same year the Russians announced their willingness to co-operate with the U.S.A. in the field of nuclear disarmament. Neither side was sincere in its desire to disarm, and both kept putting forward proposals as a way of embarrassing the other.

Khrushchev hoped that better relations with the U.S.A. would lead to a Western recognition of East Germany. The Russians had recognised West Germany in 1955. He also hoped for a solution to the problem of Berlin. By 1958 over two million East Germans had fled to West Germany, where the standard of living was much higher. Many of them were young and highly qualified, and East Germany's leader Walther Ulbricht was not exaggerating when he said that his country was bleeding to death. The elaborate system of fences and minefields along the frontier between East and West Germany was useless because East Germans could escape via Berlin. Under the Four Power Agreement it was possible for them to cross into the Western sectors of the city, from where they could catch a plane to West Germany.

From 1958 onwards Khrushchev sought to force the Western Powers to settle the question of Germany and Berlin by threatening to give the East Germans control of the transit routes to West Berlin. This would oblige the Western Powers to have dealings with and therefore to recognise the East German government. The Western Powers resisted this pressure, and a series of conferences culminating in Khrushchev's visit to the U.S.A. in 1959 failed to solve the problem. It was agreed that the matter would be discussed again at a Summit Conference in Paris in May 1960, but the prospects for the Summit did not look good. Khrushchev's Presidium colleagues began to criticise his policy of peaceful co-existence because it had achieved nothing.

The U2 Spyplane

Just before the Paris Summit, the Russians shot down one of the American U2 reconnaissance planes which had been overflying and photographing the U.S.S.R. from bases in Turkey, Pakistan and Norway. The pilot, Gary Powers, was captured alive. After the Americans had publicly denied that their planes overflew the U.S.S.R., Khrushchev produced the pilot at a press conference. The U2 incident ensured that the Paris Summit broke down after a short and bitter argument. Powers was later released by the Russians.

Khrushchev was glad to be able to break off a Summit that had little chance of success, but the U2 incident was an embarrassment for him because it enabled his critics in Russia and China to argue that the U.S.A. could not be trusted and that peaceful co-existence was a waste of time. The failure of his economic policies had further weakened Khrushchev's position and he badly needed a foreign policy success.

The Berlin Wall

In 1961 a new American President, John F. Kennedy, took office. Kennedy's inexperience seemed to offer Khrushchev the chance of scoring a foreign policy success. At their first Summit meeting in Vienna in June 1961 Khrushchev demanded a settlement of the Berlin problem by the end of the year. Kennedy responded by asking Congress for more money to spend on armaments and requesting his

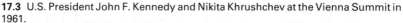

17.3 U.S. President John F. Kennedy and Nikita Khrushchev at the Vienna Summit in 1961.

17.4 Berlin, November 1961. East German workmen constructing a section of the Berlin Wall near the Brandenburg Gate. This concrete wall replaced the temporary barrier erected the previous August.

NATO allies to station more troops in Western Europe.

By June 1961 East Germans were escaping to the West via Berlin at the rate of 500 a day. 30 000 escaped in the course of July. Ulbricht demanded permission to seal off the Berlin escape route and Khrushchev agreed. In the early hours of Sunday August 13th East German forces sealed off West Berlin with road blocks and barbed wire and began hastily to construct a wall around the Western Zones of the city. Berlin was cut in two and its citizens found themselves cut off from family, friends and jobs.

The building of the Berlin Wall increased tension between the U.S.S.R. and the Western Powers. The West feared that the Russians were planning to seize West Berlin by force, and Kennedy made it clear that the U.S.A. would go to war if this happened. During the summer and autumn of 1961 there were confrontations between Soviet and Western forces along the line of the Wall. Many Western leaders, including Kennedy, visited West Berlin in the period 1962–3 to demonstrate their determination to defend the city.

Though the building of the Wall had solved a pressing problem for the East Germans, Khrushchev's policy of peaceful co-existence was in ruins and his need of a foreign policy triumph to restore his reputation was even greater.

The Cuban Missile Crisis

In 1959 left-wing guerrillas led by Fidel Castro overthrew the dictatorial regime of Fulgencio Batista in the Caribbean island of Cuba. Castro's nationalisation of the American-owned companies which controlled the island's economy angered the Americans, who rejected his request for economic aid and began to plot his downfall. Castro turned to the Russians for help and Khrushchev seized the chance of gaining an ally for the U.S.S.R. in America's backyard. In February 1960 the Russians signed a Trade Agreement with Cuba.

In April 1961 a force of 1400 anti-Communist Cuban exiles, trained and financed by the C.I.A., landed on Cuba at the Bay of Pigs with the intention of overthrowing Castro's government. They were easily defeated by Castro's forces. Fear of further American-backed attacks drove Castro into a closer relationship with the U.S.S.R. The Russians agreed to supply Cuba with arms and military equipment and by the summer of 1962 there was a sizeable Russian military presence on the island. Castro also agreed to the installation of medium and intermediate range ballistic missiles with nuclear warheads. In October 1962 the

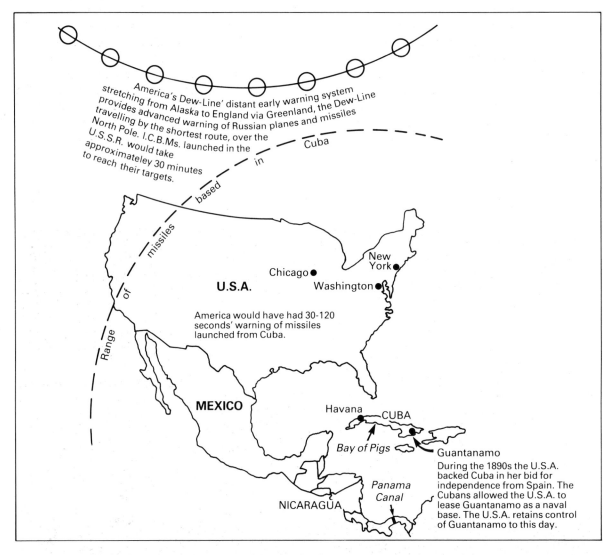

17.5 Cuban missile crisis.

Americans discovered the Russian plan to install missiles on Cuba when aerial reconnaissance revealed the whereabouts of the missile sites. There were already thirty Russian missiles on the island, though they were not yet ready for firing. Russian ships were steaming towards Cuba with more missiles on board.

Russian missiles based on Cuba would be capable of hitting all the major cities in the U.S.A. President Kennedy acted swiftly and firmly. He drew a quarantine line around Cuba and ordered the U.S. Navy to stop and search Russian ships heading for Cuba. He ordered his advisers to prepare for an invasion of Cuba and for the bombing of the missile sites. This tough approach convinced Khrushchev that Kennedy was prepared to go to war over the issue, and Khrushchev ordered the Russian ships to turn back. On October 28th he agreed to remove the missiles that were already in Cuba.

Historians disagree about why Khrushchev tried to place the missiles on Cuba. Doing so certainly gave the lie to those of his critics who said that he was being soft on the U.S.A. Had the plan succeeded it would have restored Khrushchev's credit in the Presidium. He was concerned about the 'missile-gap' that existed between the U.S.S.R. and the U.S.A., and knew that by installing medium and intermediate range missiles on Cuba he was narrowing that gap without having to go to the expense of building long-range missiles. He may have wanted to use the missiles as a bargaining counter, promising to withdraw them from Cuba if the Americans would recognise East Germany. Whatever his motives, the result was a personal disaster for him and the crisis contributed to his downfall in 1964.

Both sides learned lessons from the Cuban Missile Crisis. The Russians learned that their navy was not large enough to enable them to dominate an area so far from home, and Khrushchev and Kennedy both realised that such crises were a threat to world peace. In 1963 a 'hotline' teleprinter link was set up between the Kremlin and the White House, so that the Russian and American leaders could communicate quickly and directly in future crises. In August 1963 a Test Ban Treaty was signed by the two countries, in which both promised not to test nuclear weapons in the atmosphere, under water, or in outer space.

17.6 The U.S.S. Barry (foreground) inspecting the Soviet freighter Anosov on November 10th 1962. The Anosov was carrying a cargo of military equipment, including missiles, from Cuba back to the U.S.S.R.

Khrushchev on the Cuban Missile Crisis

Khrushchev himself explained his reasons for attempting to place Russian missiles on Cuba like this:

'The main thing was that the installation of our missiles in Cuba would, I thought, restrain the United Nations from precipitous military action against Castro's government. In addition to protecting Cuba, our missiles would have equalised what the West likes to call "the balance of power". The Americans had surrounded our country with military bases and threatened us with nuclear weapons and now they would learn what it feels like to have enemy missiles pointing at you.'

In his memoirs Khrushchev managed to make the Missile Crisis sound like a Russian success:

'As tensions rose to the point where war might break out, our countries resorted to secret diplomacy. We maintained contact with President Kennedy through his brother Robert. He came to our embassy and expressed, on behalf of the President, a desire to reach an agreement. He also consented to transmit our demands to the President. Our position was this: we would withdraw our missiles from Cuba on condition that the United States would make a public statement, pledging not to invade Cuba and promising to restrain the allies from doing so. . . . We behaved with dignity and forced the U.S.A. to demobilize and to recognize Cuba. . . . Cuba still exists today as a result of the correct policy conducted by the Soviet Union when it rebuffed the United States. I'm proud of what we did.'

Questions

(1) Why had Khrushchev good reason to fear 'precipitous military action' against Cuba by the U.S.A.?
(2) What justification did Khrushchev have for saying that the U.S.A. 'had surrounded our country with military bases'?
(3) The second paragraph is a clever attempt to present a defeat as a diplomatic triumph for the U.S.S.R. Khrushchev does this without resorting to lies, though his version of events is selective and his use of language very careful. Pick out and write down the words and phrases in the passage with which he creates the impression that he was negotiating with Kennedy from a position of strength and that the outcome of the crisis was a success for the U.S.S.R.

Sources

1st para: Khrushchev, N. S. *Khrushchev Remembers,* André Deutsch Ltd., 1971, p. 494. 2nd para: Khrushchev, N. S., *Khrushchev Remembers – The Last Testament,* André Deutsch Ltd., 1974, pp. 511–12.

18 The U.S.S.R. since 1964

The new leaders

Khrushchev was replaced not by a single leader but by a collective leadership. The new General Secretary was Leonid Brezhnev. Born in 1906, Brezhnev trained as an engineer and joined the Communist Party in 1931. Thanks to the Purges, he achieved rapid promotion in the Party. During the War he served as a political commissar with the Red Army, and after the War he became Party Chief in Moldavia and later in Kazakhstan. The new Premier, Alexei Kosygin, was born in Leningrad in 1904 and had been one of Zhdanov's closest colleagues. In the course of the next ten years Brezhnev emerged as the strong man of the government, though he never enjoyed the degree of personal power achieved by Khrushchev. His position as General Secretary meant that, like Stalin and Khrushchev before him, he was able to promote his supporters to key positions in the Party.

The new leaders began by sweeping away many of the changes that Stalin and Khrushchev had introduced since 1945. The Presidium was

18.1 November 1966. From left to right: Leonid Brezhnev, Alexei Kosygin and Nikolai Podgorny (President of the U.S.S.R. from late 1965 to 1977) watching a parade in Red Square with a group of children.

renamed the Politburo. The Sovnarkhoz system was abolished, as was the division of the Party administration into industrial and agricultural wings. The new leaders were determined that the government should have a stability that it had lacked under Khrushchev. Experienced men were allowed to remain in their jobs much longer, though this meant that the leadership was increasingly elderly. Khrushchev's aim of achieving 'Communism in our lifetime' was quietly abandoned because it was unattainable.

The emergence of Brezhnev

In 1967 Brezhnev was able to promote a close ally, Yuri Andropov, into the important post of head of the K.G.B. (Secret Police). In the same year he increased defence spending, thus winning the approval of the Army. From 1966 onwards he took a more active part in foreign policy. By 1973 he was strong enough to have some of his opponents ousted from the Politburo, and in 1977 he succeeded Nikolai Podgorny as President. Brezhnev's control of the Politburo was never as complete as Stalin's and he was probably outvoted on several important issues. Ill-health also limited his authority. When Kosygin resigned as Premier in 1980, Brezhnev was able to secure the appointment of Nikolai Tikhonov, one of his own supporters.

The Kosygin Reforms

Though Brezhnev and his colleagues shared Khrushchev's desire to produce more consumer goods and to improve the living standards of the Russian people, they used different methods. In the late 1960s Kosygin experimented with the idea of giving factory managers more freedom to use their own initiative. Instead of factories delivering the produce to the State they would sell it to State Purchasing Agencies, who might refuse to buy the goods if they were of poor quality. Factories were allowed to keep 40% of their profits and to invest the money in new machinery. The Kosygin Reforms, as this experiment became known, were a step back towards Capitalism. Because of this many

members of the Party, including Brezhnev, disapproved of them. The Reforms were abandoned after 1970. Brezhnev took the initiative away from factory managers and gave it instead to groups of factories called Industrial Associations. The success of this experiment, which began in 1973 was slight. The Russian economy remained burdened by a vast and over-powerful bureaucracy.

A Planned Economy

The eighth Five Year Plan (1966–70) was successful in promoting industrial growth (output rose by 50%) but less successful in agriculture. Poor harvests in two of the five years did not help, but even in the good years the growth in output remained low. The industrial targets of the ninth Five Year Plan were almost achieved, though performance in the consumer goods sector was disappointing. Agriculture remained a problem. Poor harvests in 1972 and 1975 forced the Russians to depend on grain imported from the U.S.A. and Canada. Self-sufficiency in food was one of the main aims of the tenth Five Year Plan (1976–80) but the results were disappointing. The rate of industrial growth slowed down. The Plan also included the ambitious scheme to build a 3500 kilometre branch line from the Trans-Siberian Railway to open up the mineral-rich areas of Siberia. The new line, known as the Baikal-Amur Railway (BAM for short) was due to be completed in 1985.

At the 26th Party Congress in 1981 Brezhnev reviewed the successes and failures of the tenth Plan and Premier Tikhonov announced the details of the eleventh Five Year Plan (1981–5). Brezhnev explained the reasons for the disappointing performance of industry under the tenth Plan. These included a shortage of skilled labour, alcoholism, absenteeism and lack of effort on the part of the workforce, pilfering and corruption, and the inefficiency of the great number of civil servants who tried to plan and control the economy. In agriculture, output had increased though poor harvests had made it impossible to meet the Plan's targets and there was no sign of the large-scale investment that had been made in machinery, fertilisers and

18.2 Part of the turbogenerator shop of the Leningrad ELECTROSILA machine building works, where units for atomic power stations are built. This photograph was taken in 1972.

drainage bearing fruit. The Collective Farm system with its huge farms and poorly-motivated peasants had hampered growth. Tikhonov emphasised that the eleventh Plan would only succeed if the U.S.S.R. could make more efficient use of her human and natural resources. The view, expressed by some Western writers, that the Soviet economy was 'on the verge of collapse' in the early 1980s was exaggerated. A report published by the C.I.A. in 1982 pointed out that the U.S.S.R. had enjoyed an average annual growth rate of 4·8% over the period 1950–80, and that the low growth rates of the late 1970s were largely attributable to bad harvests.

The living standards of Soviet citizens improved considerably in the period 1964–84. Collective Farm workers were included in the Welfare State, though they received benefits lower than those given to industrial workers. The gap in wages and living standards between urban and Collective Farm workers narrowed. The diet of ordinary Russians improved, and meat, eggs and dairy products became more widely available. Rents and the cost of living continued to be heavily subsidised by the government, as the figures on page 147 show, and the cost of living rose by an annual average of 1% between 1960 and 1980. By the time of Brezhnev's death in 1982 most Soviet families owned a T.V. set, a refrigerator and a washing machine, though only a minority owned cars. There was still an acute shortage of housing. In 1977 the average living space per person was 12.3 square metres.

Recent Five Year Plans

	1976–80 Target % growth	1976–80 Actual % growth
Heavy Industry	38–42	26
Consumer Goods	30–32	21
Agriculture	14–17	9

The Eleventh Five Year Plan Targets, % growth (1981–5)

Heavy Industry	26–28
Consumer Goods	27–29
Agriculture	12–14

Living standards

What counts is not how much you get paid, but what the money will buy.

Number of minutes you need to work to earn the money to buy 1 kilogram (1976) if earning the average wage

	Moscow	Washington	London
White bread	20	21	10
Beef	144	66	166
Potatoes	7	8	23
Bus fare (3 km)	4	6	8

Number of hours you would need to work at average wage to pay for (1976)

	Moscow	Washington	London
A month's rent for a flat	9.9	46.5	48.5
A Colour T.V.	780.0	85.6	221.6

Source
Lane, D. Politics and Society in the U.S.S.R., Martin Robertson, 1978, p. 291.

Religions and Nationalities

Khrushchev's successors remained hostile to religion, though they did not persecute the churches so actively. The majority of the clergy of the Orthodox and Baptist churches accepted the rules laid down by the government and provided the authorities with lists of church members. Religious education remained forbidden, though parents might instruct their children privately. Churches were not allowed to engage in charitable work. The government argued that it was not necessary for them to do so. Some of the clergy refused to accept these restrictions and defied the State by operating unregistered churches. Pastor Georgi Vins, the leader of the unregistered Baptists, spent much of the 1970s in prison but was permitted to leave the U.S.S.R. in 1979. Islam increased in importance in the period 1964–84, and the growth of Islamic secret societies was a particular worry to the government. The traditional Russian prejudice against the Jews remained strong. From 1967 many Jews agitated for permission to emigrate to Israel. The government allowed a limited emigration, partly

18.3 A modern apartment building in the Kalinin Prospekt, Moscow. The Church of St. Simeon Stylites on the right of the picture, which is no longer used for worship, is a museum.

as a way of improving relations with the U.S.A., and between 1970 and 1980 over 120 000 Jews left the U.S.S.R.

Though the birth rate among Great Russians was low in the 1970s, other nationalities were rapidly increasing in numbers. It was estimated that there would be 100 000 000 Islamic peoples in the U.S.S.R. by the year 2000. The Great Russians were in danger of becoming a minority. In the Central Asian regions of the U.S.S.R. only a third of the population spoke Russian. Khrushchev's and Brezhnev's hope that a single 'Soviet' nationality would emerge appeared to be misplaced. Nationalist feelings remained strong in areas such as Georgia, the Ukraine, the Baltic Republics and Central Asia.

The Dissidents

Russian writers and artists hoped that the degree of freedom that they had enjoyed under Khrushchev would be extended by his successors, but by the end of the 1960s the government had returned to a policy of strict censorship and the encouragement of socialist realism. Works that criticised Stalin were withdrawn from publication, and Brezhnev gradually rebuilt Stalin's reputation. A statue was put up by his grave and official speeches emphasised his greatness as a war leader.

Writers who were no longer able to publish their work circulated it illegally in the form of typewritten *samizdat* copies. Alexander Solzhenitsyn was deported from the U.S.S.R. in 1974. Solzhenitsyn had angered the authorities by sending writings critical of the Soviet system, including the first part of 'The Gulag Archipelago', for publication in the West.

Since 1964 Dissidents – those Soviet citizens who voice their disapproval of the government– have been treated with increasing harshness. In the late 1970s it was estimated that some 10 000 Russian men and women were in prisons, camps or psychiatric hospitals in the U.S.S.R. because of their political or religious beliefs. The trial and imprisonment of the two Dissident writers Andrei Sinyavsky and Yuli Daniel in 1966 did not deter other Dissidents from expressing their views. From 1968 a samizdat magazine, the 'Chronicle of Current Events' published details

of the government's persecution of Dissidents. Many of its contributors were arrested by the K.G.B. in 1972. Under the Helsinki Agreement of 1975 the Russian government promised to honour human rights and civil liberties, but those like Yuri Orlov who attempted to monitor the government's behaviour to see if this promise was kept were arrested and given long prison sentences. In 1980 the Nobel Prize winning physicist, Andrei Sakharov was exiled to the city of Gorky. He had signed a document protesting against the Russian invasion of Afghanistan.

Though the Dissident movement was repressed, the government did permit newspapers, magazines and broadcasting (all of which were under government control) to criticise corruption and inefficiency within the state and the Communist Party. The great majority of Soviet citizens disapproved of the Dissidents. The government was careful to emphasise their links with the West and thus to make them appear as traitors. The majority of the Dissidents had little or no admiration for Western capitalism. They believed that it was possible to operate a Communist system without

18.4 Alexander Solzhenitsyn, Moscow 1971.

the cruelty and repression that characterised the government of the U.S.S.R., and they regarded themselves as a 'loyal opposition' to that government. Ordinary citizens, provided that they kept any doubts that they had about the Soviet system to themselves, had little to fear in the years 1953–84. The massive and random terror of Stalin's time no longer operated.

Yuri Vladimirovich Andropov and Konstantin Chernenko

Leonid Brezhnev died in November 1982, aged 75. His latter years had been marred by economic disappointments and by corruption scandals involving his family and friends. Brezhnev had hoped that his successor would be Konstantin Ustinovich Chernenko, a close colleague of his since the 1940s, but the Politburo opted for a new style of leadership by electing Yuri Vladimirovich Andropov, who had been head of the K.G.B. from 1967 to 1982, to the post of General Secretary. Andropov, who became President of the U.S.S.R. in 1983,

showed signs of being a vigorous reformer. He attacked corruption within the Party and the government and called for greater discipline and efficiency in industry and agriculture. In August 1983 Andropov was taken ill, and he died in February 1984. Four days after his death the appointment of Konstantin Ustinovich Chernenko as General Secretary was announced. Chernenko, who was born into a Siberian peasant family in 1911, joined the Party and became a specialist in 'agitprop' (agitation and propaganda). During the war he helped to organise the relocation of factories evacuated from the western U.S.S.R., and after the war he worked as a Party official in Moldavia, where he became the friend and protégé of Leonid Brezhnev, who later secured Chernenko's promotion to the Politburo. In choosing as General Secretary an elderly man of uncertain health the Politburo passed over younger men such as Mikhail Gorbachev and Grigori Romanov. It remained to be seen whether Chernenko would be anything more than the spokesman of a collective leadership.

18.5 Yuri Vladimirovich Andropov (1914–1984). As head of the K.G.B. from 1967–82, Andropov played a leading part in the repression of the Dissidents.

18.6 Konstantin Chernenko, who succeeded Andropov as General Secretary in February 1984.

19 Soviet foreign policy since 1964

Détente

The word 'détente' comes from the French 'détendre', which means to slacken or relax, as an archer slackens the tension in his bowstring. Khrushchev's successors sought to take some of the tension out of East–West relations. Their policy of Détente did not mean an end to the rivalry between the Communist and non-Communist worlds, nor an end to the arms race, but they were anxious to avoid dangerous military confrontations with the U.S.A.

The U.S.S.R. and Eastern Europe – the Prague Spring

In 1968 Alexander Dubcek replaced Antonin Novotny as leader of the Czechoslovak Communist Party. Dubcek hoped to reform the Party and government, and from February 1968 he allowed the Czech people freedom to criticise the way in which the country was governed. This freedom aroused hopes of reforms more sweeping than Dubcek intended. In June Dubcek issued a proclamation which implied that free elections in which other political parties could put up candidates against the Communists would be held.

These developments, known in the West as 'the Prague Spring' – alarmed the Russians. In mid July Russia and the other members of the Warsaw Pact sent a document called 'the Warsaw Letter' to the Czech government. The letter made it clear that the Russians regarded Dubcek's liberalisation of Czechoslovakia as a threat to the Warsaw Pact. Dubcek tried to reassure them that Czechoslovakia would remain a loyal member of the Pact but the Russians, recalling the Hungarian crisis of 1956, feared that public opinion might drive Dubcek into further reforms. On August 20th Warsaw Pact forces invaded Czechoslovakia. Dubcek and his colleagues were arrested and taken to Moscow.

19.1 Prague, August 25th 1968. Young Czechs blocking the path of Soviet tanks.

There was little fighting, but the Czechs' display of passive resistance was so impressive that the Russians felt it wise to release Dubcek and the other leaders. The reforms that they had introduced were abolished and in April 1969 a new government was set up under Gustav Husak, a leading Czech Communist on whom the Russians felt that they could rely. In the 1970s Husak followed the Russian example of treating Dissidents harshly. Many members of the 'Charter 77' movement, who were demanding that the Czech government put into practice the freedoms and rights guaranteed by the Czech constitution, were imprisoned.

The Western Powers, the Chinese and the Rumanians condemned the invasion of Czechoslovakia. Brezhnev justified his action in a statement in November 1968 which became known as the 'Brezhnev Doctrine'. He argued that if Czechoslovakia had ceased to be a Commmunist state the security of all the states in the Warsaw Pact would have been threatened. Therefore the Pact members had the right to intervene to keep Czechoslovakia within the 'Socialist Commonwealth'.

Yugoslavia

Under Tito's leadership the Yugoslavs had remained outside the Warsaw Pact. Brezhnev and Kosygin tried to keep on friendly terms with the Yugoslavs and to increase trading links between the two countries. When Tito died in May 1980 there were fears in the West that Russia might take the opportunity to reassert her authority over Yugoslavia. Instead the Russians adopted a 'wait and see' policy, knowing that Yugoslavia's dependence on Russian oil was bound to drive the Yugoslavs into a closer relationship with the U.S.S.R.

Poland

Strikes and riots by Polish workers protesting against food prices brought down Gomulka's government in 1970. His successor, Eduard Gierek, tried to raise living standards by borrowing money from the West, but inflation and the shortcomings of Polish agriculture (which had never been collectivised) forced him

19.2 Lech Walesa addressing a meeting in June 1981. Walesa was awarded the Nobel Peace Prize in 1983.

to announce further price increases in 1976. The strikes and riots that met this announcement were so alarming that Gierek withdrew the price increases in order to restore order.

The election of a Polish Cardinal, Karol Wojtyla, as Pope John Paul II in 1978 further strengthened the influence of the Roman Catholic Church in Poland. Gierek welcomed John Paul on a visit to Poland in June 1979. A year later he was forced to announce further price increases. Strikes broke out all over Poland, and the workers demanded not only higher pay but the right to form independent Trade Unions. By the end of August 1980 Gierek's government had conceded this and had also relaxed censorship and permitted the broadcasting of religious services. The independent Trade Union 'Solidarity' was set up, with Lech Walesa, the leader of the militant shipyard workers of Gdansk, as its chairman. In September 1980 Gierek was replaced as First Secretary by Stanislaw Kania. Kania was unable to contain Solidarity's demands for free elections and the right of opposition parties to exist, and in October 1981 he was replaced by General Jaruzelski.

The Russians viewed these developments in Poland with alarm. Poland is of great strategic importance because it lies between the U.S.S.R. and East Germany. Many Western observers believed that the Russians would invade Poland rather than permit the situation to deteriorate any further, but Brezhnev seems to have calculated that an invasion would result in massive bloodshed and would create more problems than it would solve. He left it to Jaruzelski to deal with the crisis. In December 1981 Jaruzelski imposed martial law in Poland and arrested Walesa and other Solidarity leaders. Walesa was released a year later, and martial law was ended in 1983, but the situation in Poland remained tense.

Freedom of action within the Warsaw Pact

The Hungarian, Czech and Polish crises might give the impression that Eastern Europe was under the rigid control of the U.S.S.R. In reality Russia allows the Communist rulers of Eastern Europe some initiative. All the satellite states

belong to COMECON. This means accepting an economic strategy which keeps them reliant on the U.S.S.R., but they remain free to trade with and borrow money from the West and they are not obliged to run their economies along Russian lines. The economies of Poland and Hungary, for example, operate very differently from that of the U.S.S.R. The Rumanians, under the leadership of Nicolai Ceaucescu, who became First Secretary in 1965, refused to co-operate with some aspects of COMECON policy. Ceaucescu condemned the Russian invasion of Czechoslovakia, refused to join in Warsaw Pact military manoeuvres, and cultivated relationships with the U.S.A. and China. He was allowed to get away with this partly because Brezhnev realised that there was no danger of counter-revolution in Rumania, and partly because Rumania does not share common frontiers with NATO countries. It is much more important to the Russians to ensure that the governments of 'front line' states like East Germany and Czechoslovakia are obedient to Moscow.

Relations with China

Brezhnev and Kosygin tried to heal the breach between Russia and China, but Mao rejected suggestions that they should co-operate more closely in the Vietnam War and condemned the Russian invasion of Czechoslovakia in 1968.

In March 1969 a border conflict broke out between Russia and China in the Far East. The first incident was on Damansky Island in the Ussuri River. The fighting brought the two countries close to all-out war, and the Russians sent massive reinforcements to the Far East. There were further clashes in 1972 and 1974. As a result of the 1969 crisis both Russia and China sought to isolate each other diplomatically. The Russians continued to build up friendships with India and North Vietnam, while the Chinese worked for better relations with Japan and the E.E.C. countries and both sides tried to improve their relations with the U.S.A. The death of Mao in 1976 made no immediate difference to the quarrel between Russia and China, but the new leaders who emerged in China did not share Mao's belief that the Russians were 'revisionists'. In 1979 they agreed to have talks to improve relations between the two countries, but the talks were wrecked by the Russian invasion of Afghanistan, which alarmed the Chinese. By 1983 there were slight signs of an improvement in relations between Russia and China.

The U.S.S.R. and the Third World

Brezhnev and Kosygin continued Khrushchev's policy of winning friends for the U.S.S.R. in the Third World. Russia's hopes of 'leapfrogging' the Western Pacts that surrounded her were realised. By the end of the 1970s both SEATO and CENTO had collapsed. In their competition with the Chinese for influence in the Third World the Russians, because of their superior economic strength, emerged as the clear winners. Their hopes of acquiring bases in strategically important areas were only partially realised.

South-East Asia

After the Cuban Missile Crisis Khrushchev was anxious not to upset the U.S.A. any further, and reduced Russian aid to the Communist government of North Vietnam. Brezhnev and Kosygin reversed this policy, supporting the North Vietnamese in their war against South Vietnam and her American ally. The Vietnam War ended in a peace settlement in 1973 under which the Americans withdrew from South Vietnam. Within two years the North Vietnamese had conquered South Vietnam and in 1976 the two countries were united as a single Communist state. In 1978 Vietnam joined COMECON and signed a Friendship Treaty with the U.S.S.R. Vietnam was by then the strongest state in South East Asia and a valuable ally for Russia in her confrontation with China. The Vietnamese attacked the neighbouring state of Kampuchea (Cambodia) in December 1978 and overthrew the pro-Chinese Khmer Rouge government. In February 1979 the Chinese retaliated by attacking Vietnam, and the

Russians were forced to come to the aid of their ally. Russian threats persuaded the Chinese to back down.

Southern and Central Asia

The Russians continued to support India, though they were reluctant to support the Indians in wars against Pakistan because they did not wish to drive Pakistan into the Chinese camp. When war broke out between India and Pakistan in 1965 Kosygin acted as mediator and, at a conference at Tashkent in the U.S.S.R., persuaded Shastri of India and Ayub Khan of Pakistan to make peace. In the conflicts of 1971, in the course of which East Pakistan broke away to form the independent state of Bangladesh, Russia supported India. Russian aid to India in the 1970s took the form of loans, supplies of food and the launching of two communications satellites. On balance the Indians benefited far more from the relationship than the Russians.

In the 1970s Russia managed temporarily to improve relations with two CENTO members, Turkey and Iran. The quarrel between Turkey and the U.S.A. over the Turkish invasion of Cyprus in 1974 made possible an improvement in Russo-Turkish relations, but in September 1980 a right-wing military government came to power in Turkey and Turkish foreign policy returned to a pro-American line. Russia achieved closer trading relations with Iran in the 1970s, but in January 1979 the Shah of Iran was forced into exile. The new Islamic government, dominated by the Ayatollah Khomeini, closed down American bases on the Iranian-Soviet border but also cut off trade between Iran and the U.S.S.R. The CENTO alliance collapsed in 1979 as a result of the Iranian Revolution, but the growth of the Islamic movement worried the Russians, who have a large and growing Islamic population of their own.

In 1978 Marxists seized power in Afghanistan. Despite considerable Russian help they were unable to keep the country under control. They faced opposition from unruly hill tribesmen and Islamic rebels. In December 1979 Soviet troops moved into Afghanistan. The Russians' excuse was that the Afghan President, Hafizollah Amin, had requested assistance from them, but

19.3 Afghanistan, April 1980. Jubilant Mujaheddin freedom fighters on a captured Soviet Armoured Personnel Carrier.

Amin was murdered and replaced by Babrak Karmal, a Marxist leader whom the Russians regarded as more reliable. From 1979 onwards the Russians were involved in a costly war in Afghanistan against Islamic rebels, the Mujaheddin. Many in the West saw the Russian involvement in Afghanistan as a clear example of Soviet aggression, though it could also be interpreted as evidence of the Russians' concern to have friendly governments in their immediate vicinity.

The Middle East and Africa

In the 1960s Russia's continuing support for Egypt paid off. Russia re-armed the Egyptians after their defeat in the 1967 Six Day War with Israel and in return Nasser gave the Russians the use of naval and air bases in Egypt. This advantage was short-lived. Nasser died in 1970

and his successor, Anwar Sadat, was not satisfied with the 1971 Friendship Treaty in which the Russians promised to defend Egypt if she was attacked. Sadat was frustrated that the Russians would not give the Egyptians sufficient military aid to enable them to beat Israel. Brezhnev knew that the U.S.A. would never permit the defeat of Israel and it suited him to keep the Middle East crisis simmering so that the Arabs would have to go on relying on Russian aid. In 1973 Sadat launched the 'Yom Kippur' war against Israel without the approval of the Russians. Brezhnev was angry, but backed the Egyptians, even to the point of suggesting that Soviet forces should interpose themselves between the Egyptian and Israeli armies. That suggestion alarmed U.S. President Richard Nixon to the extent that on October 25th 1973 he put America's nuclear forces on a Stage Three Alert. The war ended in an Israeli victory. In 1976 Sadat tore up the Friendship

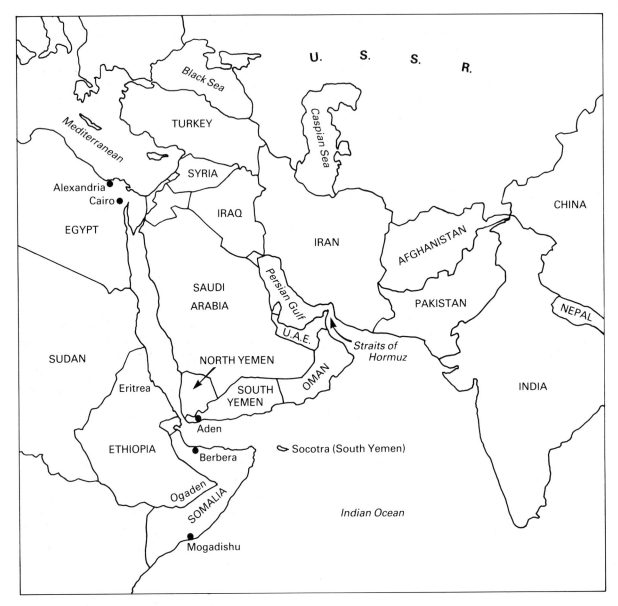

19.4 The Near East.

Treaty and expelled the Russians from their
bases in Egypt. From then until his assassination
in 1981 he enjoyed close relations with the
U.S.A. and worked to achieve the Camp David
peace agreement between Egypt and Israel in
1978. Russia was forced to look for friends
amongst the more militant Arab governments,
such as those of Syria, Iraq and Libya. The
Russians signed a Friendship Treaty with the
Iraqis in 1972. During the 1970s they worked to
maintain peace between Iran and Iraq because
they wished to be on friendly terms with both
countries, but in 1980 war broke out between
them. Brezhnev warned the Western Powers not
to get involved and cut back on Russian arms
supplies to Iraq. The internal strife in the
Lebanon in the early 1980s was a new source of
tension between the superpowers, with the

forces of Russia's ally Syria and of America's ally Israel both occupying Lebanese territory.

When the British withdrew from South Yemen in 1967 the Marxist National Liberation Front seized power. Russia built up a close relationship with the new government, backing them in a war with North Yemen in 1979. In return the Russians were allowed the use of the important naval base at Aden. From 1979 Brezhnev worked to encourage a scheme to unite North and South Yemen into a single state. South Yemen was a useful base for the Russians, from which they intervened in the Horn of Africa and in neighbouring states like Oman.

The Russians have won friends in many parts of Africa by supplying military aid, but for strategic reasons they have taken a special interest in two areas – the Horn of Africa and Southern Africa. From the late 1960s they built up a friendship with Somalia, and by a treaty of 1974 were given the use of naval bases at Berbera and Mogadishu. In 1974 a revolution in Ethiopia brought a Marxist government into power. Russia hoped to enjoy friendly relations with both Ethiopia and Somalia, but the two countries disputed the frontier region of the Ogaden and in 1977 war broke out between them. The Somalis expelled the Russians from their bases in November of that year, and the Russians sided with Ethiopia, sending Cuban military advisers to assist the Ethiopian war effort.

The civil war that broke out in the former Portuguese colony of Angola in 1975 gave the Russians a chance to intervene in Southern Africa. In 1976 they signed a Friendship Treaty with the left-wing M.P.L.A. (Movement for the Liberation of Angola) and Russian aid, which included a force of 20 000 Cuban 'military advisers', enabled the M.P.L.A. to defeat the anti-Communist UNITA forces and dominate most of Angola. In 1977 the Russians signed a Friendship Treaty with Mozambique, another former Portuguese colony with a Marxist government. Black nationalist resentment of the white-dominated government of South Africa seemed likely to give the Russians further opportunities of spreading their influence in Southern Africa.

Russian activity in the Middle East and Africa alarmed the Western Powers. The West depends heavily on supplies of oil from the Persian Gulf, much of which travels by tanker through the Red Sea and the Suez Canal or round the Cape of Good Hope. Many Western experts saw the Russian interest in Iraq, Yemen, Somalia, Ethiopia and Southern Africa as part of a strategic plan to gain control of these vital supply routes.

Latin America and the Caribbean

Russia's friendship with Cuba was strained by the Missile Crisis because Castro was angered by the withdrawal of the Russian missiles. By the late 1960s friendly relations had been restored, though Castro was impatient with the Russians because they would not support his schemes for spreading revolution to other states in the Caribbean and Latin America. Cuba became a member of COMECON in 1972 and continued to depend on large-scale Soviet economic aid. During the 1970s Cuban troops fought on behalf of the U.S.S.R. in the Yemen, Ethiopia and Angola.

In 1970 a Marxist, Salvador Allende, was elected President of Chile. This gave the Russians the opportunity of building an alliance with a mainland Latin American state, but they ignored the chance because at the time they were anxious to improve their relations with the U.S.A. Russian aid to the Allende government remained niggardly, and when the Allende government was overthrown in 1973 as a result of an American-backed coup the Russians made only a token protest.

The U.S.A. remained sensitive about Russian military involvement in Cuba. In 1979 President Carter demanded that the Russians withdraw a Combat Brigade which they had stationed on the island. Brezhnev refused to do so. In the same year a revolution in Nicaragua overthrew the American-backed Somoza regime. Left-wing Sandinista guerrillas seized control of the country. In the years that followed American hostility and suspicion drove the Sandinistas into a closer relationship with the U.S.S.R. This pattern could be repeated in many other states in Central and Southern America. Russia has, thanks to her Cuban ally, a foothold in the region and is likely to exploit any tensions that arise.

The global policy of the U.S.S.R.

Russian foreign policy can be made to sound very alarming, especially when the growth of the Russian Navy is taken into account. During the 1970s the Russians benefited from the fact that American foreign policy was in disarray. Their failure in Vietnam made the Americans reluctant to get involved in other conflicts against Communism, and the Russians were able to win influence in a number of areas. It is important to remember that they suffered some setbacks, including the loss of their bases in Egypt and Somalia, and that their experience with India has shown how difficult it is to turn an aid-relationship into a useful and manageable alliance. The American tendency to back repressive dictatorships such as the Somoza regime in Nicaragua has helped the Russians to find opportunities of gaining influence.

Relations with the U.S.A.

Relations between Russia and the U.S.A. remained poor for several years after the Cuban Missile Crisis. The Vietnam War, the 1967 Arab-Israeli War and the Czechoslovak crisis of 1968 helped to keep the two countries at loggerheads and during this time the Russians built up their stock of nuclear weapons until they achieved a rough equality with the U.S.A. Brezhnev and Kosygin were anxious to reduce tensions between the two countries. They had no wish to see a further round in the arms race, and they needed to import high-technology goods from the U.S.A. in order to develop Russian industry. They also hoped to achieve a Western recognition of East Germany, and they wished to avoid dangerous confrontations between East and West. In 1969 President Nixon indicated a willingness to discuss the limitation of strategic

19.5 Leonid Brezhnev (left) and U.S. President Richard Nixon (right) raise their glasses at a meeting in the White House in 1973.

nuclear weapons and in 1970 the Strategic Arms Limitation Talks (SALT) began. The talks led to a treaty, SALT 1, signed in 1972. SALT 1 set limits to the growth in the number of long-range missiles held by both sides and was an important step in the direction of Détente.

Nixon believed that there should be a 'linkage' between arms control agreements and Russia's global behaviour. He hoped to use Russia's desire for arms control as a lever to persuade the Russians to abandon their adventurous policy in the Third World. The Russians were pursuing arms control for its own sake and regarded it as a separate issue.

Admiral Gorshkov and the rise of the Soviet Navy

Admiral Gorshkov was appointed Commander in Chief of the Soviet Navy in 1957. At first he concentrated on building up the submarine fleet, but in the 1960s he began to build up a 'blue water' navy, a surface fleet of long-distance ships which would enable the U.S.S.R. to make its influence felt around the world. By 1980 the fleet was strong enough to defend the U.S.S.R. against all possible aggressors and to engage in 'gunboat diplomacy' around the world. By 1990, if present plans are continued, it will be much more powerful.

Weapons

Military experts divide nuclear weapons into 'strategic' and 'tactical'. Strategic weapons are for a long-distance strike at the enemy heartland. Tactical weapons are for use on a localised battlefield. Some weapons, such as air-launched Cruise Missiles can be used in either way. This table shows the changing balance in Strategic weapons:

	1971	1975	1983
USA			
ICBMs	1054	1054	1045
SLBMs	656	656	568
Long-range Bombers	360	397	272
USSR			
ICBMs	1527	1527	1398
SLBMs	448	784	980
Long-range Bombers	140	135	143

(ICBM = Intercontinental Ballistic Missile, SLBM = Submarine-launched Ballistic Missile. N.B. many missiles have several warheads, known as Multiple Independently-targettable Re-entry Vehicles or MIRVS)

The balance in conventional forces (1983–4 figures)

	U.S.A. + NATO	U.S.S.R. + Warsaw Pact
Manpower in uniform	4 991 000	6 068 000
Reserve manpower	5 345 000	6 718 000
Main battle tanks	20 722	25 490
Attack submarines	182	145
Carriers	13	4
Cruisers	15	24
Bombers	34	455
Ground-attack aircraft	2 186	1 685

Figures do not tell the whole story. Professional expertise and standards of equipment are very important. Though the military balance in Europe has moved slowly but steadily in favour of the U.S.S.R. since 1960, the present situation is not one in which either side could be confident of winning, and if the war were to escalate into a strategic nuclear conflict there would be no winner.

Source
International Institute of Strategic Studies, *The Military Balance,* 1983–84.

Ostpolitik

West Germany's Chancellor Brandt wanted to establish better relations with his country's eastern neighbours. Brezhnev welcomed this 'Ostpolitik' (Eastern Policy) of Brandt's as an opportunity to reduce international tension over Berlin and to persuade the Western Powers to recognise East Germany. In 1971 the U.S.S.R., the U.S.A., Britain and France signed a Four Power Agreement which made travel between West Germany and West Berlin much easier. In December 1972 the two Germanies signed the Basic Treaty, in which they agreed to exchange Permanent Missions and to maintain friendly relations. The East Germans, who had hoped for full diplomatic recognition, were disappointed by this agreement. In 1973 both Germanies joined the United Nations and during the next five years most major Western states officially recognised the East German government.

Linkage

Nixon's visit to China in February 1972 worried the Russians and made them more anxious to get on better terms with the U.S.A. When Nixon visited Moscow in May 1972 agreements were signed under which the U.S.A. promised to lend Russia money with which to buy American high technology goods. The Yom Kippur War of 1973 (see page 115) strained relations between the two countries seriously. The U.S. Congress insisted that there should be no trade agreements with the U.S.S.R. unless the Russians allowed more Jews to emigrate, and limited U.S. loans to the U.S.S.R. to 300 000 000 dollars. The Russians, angered by this 'linkage' between a trade agreement and the question of Jewish emigration, which they felt was none of the Americans' business, cancelled the agreement in January 1975.

Helsinki

Détente took new directions after 1972. Talks began in Vienna to try to achieve Mutual and Balanced Force Reductions (M.B.F.R.) – a step by step reduction of the number of troops that both sides had stationed in Europe. By 1983 these talks had gone through nearly three hundred sessions without achieving anything. In 1973 talks began in Helsinki to prepare for a Conference on Security and Co-operation in Europe (C.S.C.E.). The C.S.C.E. took place in Helsinki in 1975. The Conference was attended by the U.S.A., the U.S.S.R., Canada, Britain and every European nation except Albania. The participants agreed to recognise the existing frontiers of Europe, to co-operate with each other economically and to guarantee human rights and civil liberties. It was agreed that they would meet again in Belgrade in 1977 to review the working of these arrangements. The human rights element in the Helsinki Final Agreement was another example of the Western Powers trying to achieve 'linkage' between Détente and Russian good behaviour.

Détente breaks down

At the Belgrade Conference U.S. President Carter took the Russians to task for their failure to respect human rights and civil liberties. The Belgrade Conference achieved little, and progress towards the signing of a second SALT agreement remained slow. The Russians could not understand Carter's insistence on 'linkage', and were alarmed by the growing relationship between the U.S.A. and China. By the time Carter and Brezhnev signed the second SALT Agreement in June 1979, relations between the U.S.A. and the U.S.S.R. had deteriorated. The Iranian and Nicaraguan Revolutions and the Cuban Combat Brigade Crisis alarmed the Americans, as did the continuing build-up of Warsaw Pact conventional forces in Europe and the Soviet deployment of mobile SS-20 missiles which began in 1977. In December 1979 NATO announced its intention of deploying Cruise Missiles in Europe. When the Russians invaded Afghanistan at Christmas in 1979, Carter placed

a temporary ban on grain exports to the U.S.S.R. and organised a boycott of the 1980 Moscow Olympic Games by some Western countries. The Americans also refused to ratify SALT 2. Détente had broken down.

The new Cold War

Ronald Reagan, who was elected President of the U.S.A. in 1980, was willing to negotiate on the limitation of nuclear weapons but believed that this was best done from a position of strength. He believed, as the extract on page 162 makes clear, that Détente had not curbed the U.S.S.R.'s expansionist ambitions. US-Soviet talks concerning the limitation of Intermediate-range nuclear forces (I.N.F.) began in Geneva in November 1981, Strategic Arms Reduction Talks (START) in June 1982.

In November 1981 he put forward the 'Zero Option', a suggestion that the U.S.S.R. should dismantle her SS-20 missiles and that NATO would, in return, cancel the planned deployment of Cruise and Pershing II missiles in Western Europe. The Soviet government rejected the Zero Option. In December 1981 Reagan reacted to the imposition of martial law in Poland by banning high technology exports to the U.S.S.R. The Russians were puzzled by this, since they had not used force in Poland. Brezhnev regretted the breakdown of Détente, a policy with which he was closely associated. He could draw some comfort from the signs of strain in the Western Alliance. Indications that the U.S.A. might be prepared to fight a limited nuclear war in Europe and the imminent arrival of Cruise missiles in Britain helped to revive peace movements in the West. The death of Brezhnev and the succession of Yuri Andropov in 1982 added a further degree of uncertainty to the situation. The shooting down of a Korean jetliner in Soviet airspace by a Russian fighter plane and the American intervention in Grenada in the autumn of 1983 further deepened tensions between the U.S.S.R. and the West. By the end of that year the M.B.F.R., I.N.F. and START talks were all deadlocked and there was a danger of a renewed arms race which the U.S.S.R. could ill afford.

Détente

The extracts below are from speeches on the subject of Détente by Soviet General Secretary Leonid Brezhnev in March 1976 and by U.S. President Ronald Reagan in January 1981. Read them carefully and then answer the questions below.

Brezhnev (1976)

'The struggle to consolidate the principles of peaceful co-existence, to assure lasting peace, and to reduce and in the long term to eliminate the danger of world war has been and remains the main element of our policy towards the capitalist states. Considerable progress has been achieved in the past five years. The passage from the Cold War, from the explosive confrontations of two worlds to Détente was primarily connected with changes in the correlation of world forces. But much effort was required for people – especially those responsible for state policies – to become accustomed to the thought that the natural state of things is not brinkmanship but negotiation, not confrontation but peaceful co-op eration. . . . . Though world peace is by no means guaranteed yet, we have every reason to declare that the improvement of the international climate is convincing evidence that lasting peace is not merely a good intention but an entirely realistic objective. And we can and must continue to work tirelessly to achieve it.'

Reagan (1981)

'So far Détente's been a one-way street which the Soviet Union has used to pursue its own aims. I know of no leader of the Soviet Union, since the Revolution and including the present leadership, that has not more than once repeated in the various Communist congresses they hold, their determination that their goal must be the promotion of world revolution and a one-world Socialist or Communist state. . . . Now, as long as they do that and as long as they, at the same time, have openly and publicly declared that the only morality they recognize is what will further their cause, meaning they reserve the right to commit any crime, to lie, to cheat in order to obtain it, I think that when you do business with them – even in Détente – you keep that in mind.'

Questions

(1) To what developments was Brezhnev referring when he said 'considerable progress has been achieved in the past five years'?

(2) Give two examples of 'explosive confrontations' which characterised the Cold War of the 1960s.

(3) What were the 'changes in the correlation of world forces' that helped to bring about Détente?

(4) What Soviet actions in the period 1976–81 made Ronald Reagan think that Détente had been a 'one way street' in which the Russians refused to abandon their plans for world revolution?

Source
Chomsky, Steele, Gittings: *Superpowers in Collision*, Pelican Books, 1982, pp. 44 and 46.

Conclusion

One person could use the facts in this chapter to portray the U.S.S.R. as an aggressive power bent on world domination. Another could depict a frightened and defensive Soviet Union. The Bear Rampant? Or the Bear at Bay? Some historians believe that the U.S.S.R. is both – as one American expert put it, there's nothing so offensive as a Russian on the defensive. Since 1917 the U.S.S.R. has become a world power, though in seeking to exert a global influence she has followed the example of the U.S.A. The question as to why she has followed the American example can be answered in several ways. Soviet rhetoric about world domination and world revolution may be sincere and may represent the long-term foreign policy aims of the U.S.S.R. The growth of the Soviet Navy, the presence of Soviet military and economic advisers in many Third World countries and the intervention of Soviet and Cuban troops in countries such as Angola and Ethiopia can be seen as evidence of this. If the Soviets are aiming at world domination, their pursuit of this aim in the past thirty years has been neither skilful nor particularly successful. It is also possible that the rhetoric about world revolution is intended largely for internal consumption in the U.S.S.R., and that the Soviet leaders are the prisoners of their own ideology, trapped into competing with the Capitalist West because if they do not do so it is more difficult for them to justify the disciplined and repressive way in which they govern their country. Since Soviet foreign policy is determined in secret by a small group of men it is difficult to be certain of its purposes. It is unlikely that the U.S.S.R. would start an all-out war against the Western Alliance, since the risks involved would be terrible, but it is probable that the Soviet government believes that the growing naval and military strength of the U.S.S.R. will give them increasing political leverage in strategic areas of the world.

20 Life in the modern U.S.S.R.

Constitution and Government

In 1977 a new constitution replaced the one issued by Stalin in 1936. Russia remains a federation of Soviet Socialist Republics, some of which are subdivided into smaller units to give minor nationalities a say in their own affairs. At each level of government from village or urban district to Republic and Union there are elected Soviets (Councils). At the top of this structure is the Supreme Soviet, the parliament of the U.S.S.R. Each Republic has its own Supreme Soviet, government and constitution, and all have the right to withdraw from the U.S.S.R., though none has so far tried to do so.

The Supreme Soviet meets twice a year for a few days and, as under the 1936 Constitution (see page 82) has two houses. All laws require a

20.1 The Supreme Soviet of the U.S.S.R. in session.

majority vote by each house. Day to day decisions are taken by two smaller bodies, both elected by the Supreme Soviet. One is the Council of Ministers, the Cabinet of the U.S.S.R. The other is the Presidium of the Supreme Soviet, a powerful body which can declare war, dismiss ministers and issue laws by decree. The top man in the Presidium of the Supreme Soviet is its President, who is the official Head of State of the U.S.S.R. The Council of Ministers, which has over a hundred members, is chaired by the Premier of the U.S.S.R.

The Constitution also guarantees Soviet citizens certain rights such as equality under the law, equality of the sexes and nationalities, the right to work, freedom of religious belief and the privacy of letters and phone calls.

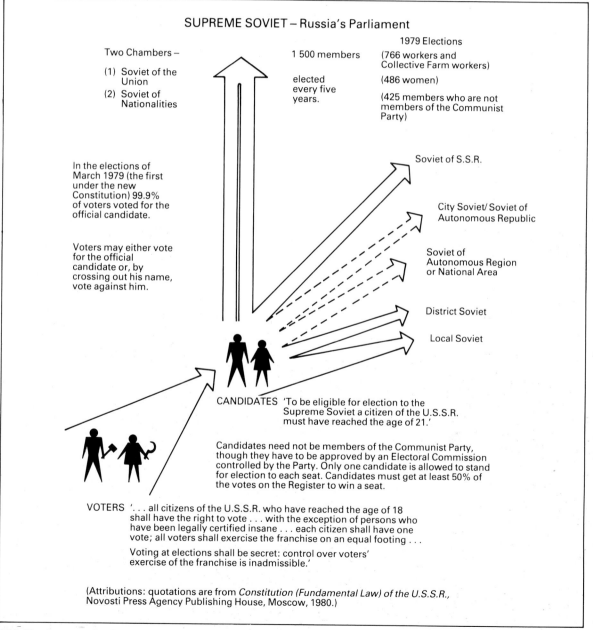

SUPREME SOVIET – Russia's Parliament

Two Chambers –

(1) Soviet of the Union
(2) Soviet of Nationalities

1 500 members

elected every five years.

1979 Elections

(766 workers and Collective Farm workers)

(486 women)

(425 members who are not members of the Communist Party)

In the elections of March 1979 (the first under the new Constitution) 99.9% of voters voted for the official candidate.

Voters may either vote for the official candidate or, by crossing out his name, vote against him.

Soviet of S.S.R.

City Soviet/ Soviet of Autonomous Republic

Soviet of Autonomous Region or National Area

District Soviet

Local Soviet

CANDIDATES 'To be eligible for election to the Supreme Soviet a citizen of the U.S.S.R. must have reached the age of 21.'

Candidates need not be members of the Communist Party, though they have to be approved by an Electoral Commission controlled by the Party. Only one candidate is allowed to stand for election to each seat. Candidates must get at least 50% of the votes on the Register to win a seat.

VOTERS '. . . all citizens of the U.S.S.R. who have reached the age of 18 shall have the right to vote . . . with the exception of persons who have been legally certified insane . . . each citizen shall have one vote; all voters shall exercise the franchise on an equal footing . . .

Voting at elections shall be secret: control over voters' exercise of the franchise is inadmissible.'

(Attributions: quotations are from *Constitution (Fundamental Law) of the U.S.S.R.*, Novosti Press Agency Publishing House, Moscow, 1980.)

20.2 The Supreme Soviet.

The **RUSSIAN SOVIET FEDERATIVE SOCIALIST REPUBLIC**
includes Siberia and the Far Eastern parts of the U.S.S.R.

20.3 Political structure of the U.S.S.R. from 1977.

Constitutional Structure of the U.S.S.R.

The 15 Soviet Socialist Republics

1. Russian Soviet Federative Socialist Republic

includes: { 16 Autonomous S.S.Rs.
5 Autonomous Regions
10 National Areas

2. Ukrainian S.S.R.
3. Byelorussian S.S.R.
4. Uzbek S.S.R. – includes: 1 Autonomous S.S.R.
5. Kazakh S.S.R.
6. Georgian S.S.R. – includes: 2 Autonomous S.S.Rs., 1 Autonomous Region
7. Azerbaijan S.S.R. – includes: 1 Autonomous S.S.R., 1 Autonomous Region
8. Lithuanian S.S.R.
9. Moldavian S.S.R.
10. Latvian S.S.R.
11. Kirghiz S.S.R.
12. Tajik S.S.R. – includes: 1 Autonomous Region
13. Armenian S.S.R.
14. Turkmen S.S.R.
15. Estonian S.S.R.

Russia's parliament, the Supreme Soviet, has two chambers. One of them, the Soviet of the Union, has 748 deputies. The other, the Soviet of Nationalities, has 750 deputies.

In the Soviet of the Union the number of deputies from each S.S.R. reflects the number of people living in that S.S.R.

In the Soviet of Nationalities every S.S.R. has 32 deputies, every Autonomous Republic has 11, every Autonomous Region has 5 and every National Area has 1.

20.4 The opening of the 25th Congress of the Communist Party of the Soviet Union in Moscow.

The Communist Party

Since membership of the Party is a route to power and privilege it may seem surprising that in the early 1980s only 7% of Russians were party members. Membership involves a considerable commitment of time and energy and most people in the U.S.S.R., like most people in Britain, are not actively engaged in politics.

The Party is dominated, especially in its upper ranks, by Great Russians and by men. It has its own structure, closely parallel to the structure of the State. At the top is the Politburo, which remains the effective policy-making body for the U.S.S.R. The most powerful official in the Party

is the General Secretary, who is usually the dominant figure in the Soviet government. The Party operates a youth movement called the Pioneers whose members receive political training and engage in outdoor pursuits. Komsomol, the Young Communist League, provides training for those who have outgrown the Pioneers. The Party operates Political Schools to train those members who will work as full-time Party officials. All the ruling bodies in the Party are elected by members but the Party operates on the Leninist system of Democratic Centralism, under which Party members are expected to obey the commands of the leadership.

The Family

Family life is valued in the U.S.S.R. Some early Communists advocated the abolition of marriage but after the Civil War it was decided to retain the existing system of marriage and child-rearing, and Stalin passed laws which made divorce more difficult. Marriage remains as popular as in the West and the divorce rate is at least as high.

Most Soviet women go out to work, though they are still expected to bear the brunt of housework and child-rearing. Many families have at least one grandparent living with them. Shortage of housing means that the size of families is much smaller than in previous generations. Roughly half of Russia's married couples have only one child. Children are allowed to inherit their parents' savings and possessions.

Education and Culture

Many Soviet children attend nursery schools because their mothers have jobs, and parents contribute a small amount to the cost of nursery schooling. All other education in the U.S.S.R. is free. Children attend primary school from the age of seven, transferring to secondary school at eleven and remaining there at least until they are fifteen. Polytechnical Secondary Schools cater for pupils who wish to learn practical industrial skills, and there are specialist schools for those who show aptitude at music, dance or mathematics.

20.5 Akademgorodok, the Soviet 'Science City' in Siberia which is a major centre of scientific research.

20.6 A classroom in Moscow's School no. 444 in 1977. This school specialises in Maths and Computer Programming.

The content of Soviet education reflects the ideas of the Communist Party. Children are taught from an early age to revere Lenin and follow his example. There is no religious education in schools and the state aims to bring children up as atheists. Corporal punishment is not allowed. Parents are held responsible for their children's behaviour and may be publicly criticised if their children are idle or break school rules.

Russia has over fifty universities and at any one time about five million students are enrolled in them. Many of these are on part-time or correspondence courses. A majority are studying practical subjects such as science and engineering. Students win their places at university by sitting an entrance exam, though their character and school record are also taken into account. In Russia, as in Western countries, the children of university-educated parents are far more likely to go to university than the children of manual workers.

The U.S.S.R. has an impressive cultural life. Classical music, theatre and ballet receive generous state support. Antiquities are carefully preserved, and the Russians take real pride in the achievements of Tsars, such as Peter the Great, who modernised and enlarged their country. The work of great writers of the past, such as Pushkin, Tolstoy and Dostoyevsky, is highly valued even though it does not follow the rules of Socialist Realism.

The Arts and the Media

The Arts in Russia have been subject to censorship since Tsarist times, though the degree of censorship has varied. In contemporary Russia creative artists are expected to be the servants of the Communist State and to reflect its ideals in their work by adopting the style of Socialist Realism (see chapter 11). Death, exile and incarceration in psychiatric hospitals have been the fates of those courageous writers and artists who have deviated from the wishes of the Soviet government.

All newspapers, radio and television stations in the U.S.S.R. are state-owned and subject to strict government control. The output of news is limited, and the authorities delay or suppress stories which reflect badly on the Communist system and emphasise the military, economic and technological successes of the U.S.S.R. and other Communist states. They also use the media to present the policies of foreign countries, especially of the U.S.A., in an unfavourable light. Russian-language broadcasts by the B.B.C. and other Western broadcasting organisations are subjected to periodic jamming.

Class and society

In theory Russia is a classless society, but in matters such as education and standard of living there are definite divisions within Soviet society. Urban workers remain better off than Collective Farm Workers. Highly qualified people are paid much more than the unqualified. Senior Party members receive privileges such as access to special shops, greater opportunities of foreign travel and possibly the use of a 'dacha', or country cottage. Cosmonauts and important artists and sportsmen share these privileges.

Work and Welfare

There is almost no unemployment in the U.S.S.R. Workers receive a guaranteed minimum wage, and welfare benefits include retirement pensions, free medical care and 112 days maternity leave. Membership of Trade Unions is technically voluntary, though 98% of the workforce belongs to them. The job of the Unions, which are Communist-controlled, is less to represent the interests of their members than to organise, discipline and train them to work effectively and meet the demands of the current Plan. Strikes are rare and when they happen it is because the Unions have failed in their task of controlling the workforce. Striking is not illegal, but strikers can be and are prosecuted under laws which forbid people to 'weaken or undermine the Soviet State'. The Unions would argue that strikes are not necessary since the interests of the workers and the interests of the State are by definition identical. Attempts to set up independent trade unions have been severely punished.

20.7 A paediatrician makes her rounds in a village hospital in 1983. Health and welfare provision in the rural U.S.S.R. improved in the period 1964–83.

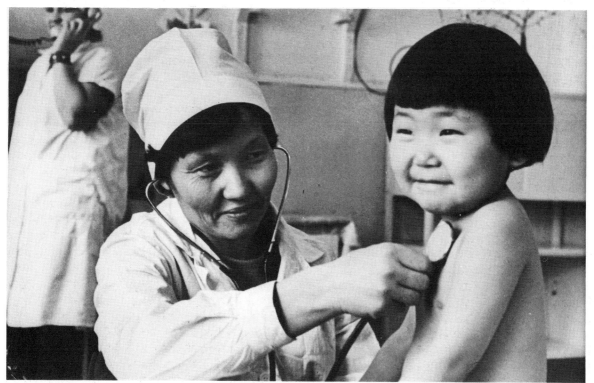

Planning in a Command Economy

Russia's is a Command Economy – the State decides what will be made or grown and fixes prices – but the government's control over the economy is far from complete. The administrative task of drawing up and running a Five Year Plan is so vast that muddle and inefficiency inevitably creep in. The system discourages initiative and effort by managers and leads to 'storming' – factories working at peak effort for part of the month in order to meet the monthly Plan target and then slacking off for the rest of the month. The fact that prices are determined by the government makes it very difficult to judge whether factories are working efficiently. The Command Economy does have advantages. It enables the Russians to carry out expensive projects, such as the BAM Railway, which are of great long-term benefit but which need massive amounts of money which private investors in a free economy would be unlikely to provide.

Shopping in a Command Economy is a hit and miss business. The shops are usually full of a limited range of goods. When Russians see a queue, their instinct is to join it, even though they do not know what is on sale. If something unusual is available people will buy for their friends as well as for themselves. Since the 1960s the Russians have developed an appetite for consumer goods. The Communist Party has misgivings about the effect of 'consumerism' on its citizens, but knows from experience in Poland that shortages of food and clothing and sudden increases in prices can create serious unrest. Recent Five Year Plans have given the manufacture of consumer goods a high priority.

20.8 Shoppers outside 'Children's World', a well-known Moscow department store.

20.9 Modern Moscow. The tall building centre-left across the bridge is the headquarters of the C.M.E.A. or COMECON.

Law and Order

In Russia the law is seen as a means of creating the perfect Communist society and the Party is therefore above the law. Pre-trial investigation is very thorough, with the result that most people who stand trial are convicted. There is no tradition of considering the accused person innocent until proven guilty, and the main job of the courts is to determine punishment. The death penalty can be applied in cases of treason, murder, large-scale theft of state property and 'speculation' or black marketeering.

Minor crimes are dealt with by Comrades Courts where the accused's workmates judge his case and have the power to fine him fifty roubles.

The law is enforced by the Militia (Police) and the Voluntary Militia – groups of Trade Unionists or Komsomols who patrol the streets to discourage street crime. Major crimes against the state are dealt with by the 500 000 strong K.G.B., which also guards Russia's frontiers and engages in espionage in foreign countries.

Hooliganism and street-crime are a problem in the larger cities, and alcoholism is a major cause of violent crime. There is a considerable degree of corruption. Goods are pilfered from state enterprises and sold 'na levo' ('on the left' or 'under the counter') and in recent years the death penalty has been used quite frequently to deter people from trading in pilfered goods.

Patriotism

The majority of Russians are deeply patriotic, and their rulers encourage them to see the outside world as hostile and aggressive. Russia is a militarised society. Military language is used to describe economic achievements ('battalions of shock-workers', 'storming the heights of the Plan') and great public occasions such as May Day are marked by displays of military might. Members of the Young Pioneers are trained in military drill. At 14 children can join D.O.S.A.A.F. (the Voluntary Committee for Assistance to the Armed Forces) and learn about weapons and tactics. All fit eighteen-year-olds do two years' military service unless they have a place at a university or polytechnic, in which case they are trained as reserve officers during their course. Sport is partly under military patronage and top athletes are part of the privileged elite of Soviet society.

Conclusion

It is impossible to know what ordinary Russians think about Communism. Only a tiny minority express their disapproval of the system openly, but the lack of freedom of expression which concerns writers and artists is probably of less interest to workers who know that they have no major worries about unemployment, sickness or old age. The rulers of the U.S.S.R. are an elite who have achieved power and privilege and they are not inclined to change a system under which they have prospered.

20.10 November 7th 1983. Leading members of the Soviet government watch the military parade to commemorate the 66th anniversary of the October Revolution. The building on which they are standing is the Lenin Mausoleum in Red Square, Moscow.

Glossary

Atheism
A definite belief that there is no God. The U.S.S.R. is officially an atheist state, and membership of the Communist Party of the Soviet Union is not compatible with religious belief.

Autocracy
A system of government in which absolute power is concentrated in the hands of one man. The Tsars of Russia were, in theory, autocrats, though the complexity of their job forced them to share power with ministers and officials.

Bourgeois
Can mean simply 'middle class', but Marx and Engels used it as a technical term. For them a bourgeois was a person who owned some of the means of production, whether in the form of factories, mines or stocks and shares. The collective noun is bourgeoisie.

Bourgeois Individualism
A type of literature of which Stalin and Zhdanov disapproved. Such literature concentrates on the inner thoughts and emotions of individual characters. 'Bourgeois individualist' is also applied as a description of people who are fashion conscious, snobbish or self-centred.

Bourgeois Revolution
The point in history when, according to Marx's and Engels' theories, the bourgeois capitalists seize power from the king and the landowning aristocracy.

Brezhnev Doctrine
The view, first put into words by Leonid Brezhnev in November 1968, that Russia should not allow countries that were 'within the Socialist Commonwealth' (i.e. countries with Communist governments) to turn away from Communism. Brezhnev argued that if they did try to abandon Communism they were a threat to the security of the U.S.S.R. and the other Communist states, who would have the right to intervene militarily to bring them back within the Communist fold. The Warsaw Pact invasion of Czechoslovakia in August 1968 is an example of the doctrine in action.

Bureaucrats
Civil servants. Tsarist Russia was noted for its large and cumbersome bureaucracy, and the Communists developed their own larger administrative machine, though successive leaders were unable to make it work efficiently.

Capitalism
The system of economic organisation in which the means of production (factories, mines etc.) are owned by private individuals. In practice most of the western countries which are referred to as 'capitalist' by the Russians have mixed economies in which some industries are state-owned.

CENTO
An alliance originally (1955–59) known as the Baghdad Pact, but renamed the Central Treaty Organisation in 1959. Its members (Britain, Turkey, Iran and Pakistan) pledged themselves to prevent the spread of Communism in the Near East. The alliance collapsed in 1979 after the Iranian revolution.

Cheka
The original name of the Communist Secret Police in Russia. Its full name was the Extraordinary Commission, and it was founded in 1918 under the leadership of Felix Dzerzhinsky.

C.M.E.A.
See under COMECON.

Collectivisation
The process by which, in the period 1929–37, the Russian peasants were organised into collective farms under state supervision.

COMECON
The Council for Mutual Economic Assistance

founded by the U.S.S.R. in 1949 to co-ordinate the economies of the Communist states of Eastern Europe with Russia's economy. Its headquarters are in Moscow.

Cominform
The Communist Information Bureau which operated from 1947–56. Its function was to keep the Communist states of Eastern Europe informed on Russian policy. Its headquarters were at first in Belgrade, and later in Bucharest.

Comintern
Otherwise known as the Third International. An international agency set up by the Russians in 1919 to co-ordinate the activities of Communist Parties throughout the world. Stalin abolished it in 1943.

Commissar
The Bolsheviks wished to avoid using the term 'minister' because of its Tsarist associations, so they referred to government ministers as 'people's commissars' during the early days of Communist rule.

Commune
The system of peasant agriculture set up by Tsar Alexander II after the abolition of serfdom in 1861 permitted peasants to own land but compelled them to farm it communally, according to the decisions of a village council formed of all the heads of households. Peter Stolypin (Prime Minister 1906–11) abolished the legal ties that bound the peasants to the communes.

Communism
Used by Marx and Engels as the word for the perfect society which they believed lay at the end of the historical process. In such a society the means of production would be owned communally. Used in a more general sense as meaning the political theories put forward by Marx and Engels and their followers.

Constituent Assembly
The democratically elected parliament whose job was to draft a new republican constitution for Russia after the abdication of the Tsar. By the time it was elected (November 1917) the Bolshevik Revolution had happened. It met briefly in January 1918 but was closed down by the Bolsheviks.

Constitutional Monarchy
A system of government in which the powers of the sovereign are limited by a written constitution or by custom, and in which an elected parliament has a share of power.

Détente
A relaxation of tension in international relations. The word is usually used to describe the relaxation of tension in the Cold War that was temporarily achieved in the early 1970s.

Dictatorship of the Proletariat
A phase of history which comes, according to the theories of Marx and Engels, after the Proletarian Revolution. During this time the last traces of the bourgeoisie are wiped out, and when this process is complete Communism will have been achieved.

Duma
The elected parliament granted by Nicholas II in 1905. The first Duma was elected in 1906. The Provisional Government of 1917 was a committee of Duma members.

G.P.U.
The Communist Secret Police was known as the G.P.U. for a time during the 1920s. See also Cheka, O.G.P.U., N.K.V.D. and K.G.B.

K.G.B.
The current name for the Secret Police in the U.S.S.R. The initials stand for Committee for State Security. The K.G.B. performs the functions that previously belonged to the Cheka, G.P.U., O.G.P.U. and N.K.V.D.

Kolkhoz
The Russian word for collective farm (see above).

Komsomol
The Young Communist League – the youth organisation of the Communist Party of the Soviet Union.

Kuomintang
The Chinese Nationalist Party, defeated by the Chinese Communists in 1949.

Machine Tractor Station
Stalin established these to provide the collective farms with tractors. Each M.T.S. had a repair depot and skilled mechanics. They were abolished by Khrushchev in the 1950s.

Narodnik
Literally means 'populist'. The Narodniks were 19th century Russian revolutionaries who hoped for a peasant revolution but found the peasants unreceptive to their ideas.

NATO
The North Atlantic Treaty Organisation – an alliance established by the Western Powers in 1949 for the defence of Western Europe.

N.K.V.D.
The Communist Secret Police (see Cheka, G.P.U., O.G.P.U., K.G.B.) was known as the N.K.V.D. (Peoples Commissariat for Internal Affairs) for much of the 1930s and 1940s.

O.G.P.U.
The Communist Secret Police (see also Cheka, G.P.U., N.K.V.D., K.G.B.).

Okhrana
The Tsarist Secret Police. Its main task was to infiltrate and destroy illegal political parties.

Orthodox
In a general sense it means holding correct views. The Orthodox Church is a branch of the Christian Church, and the majority of Russians in the 19th and early 20th centuries belonged to the Russian Orthodox Church.

Peaceful Co-existence
The term applied to Nikita Khrushchev's attempt to secure better relations between Russia and the West in the late 1950s and early 1960s.

Personality Cult
A propaganda campaign designed to make people feel respect for a leader, living or dead.

Personality cults of different kinds were developed around Stalin and Brezhnev.

Pogrom
A massacre of Jews in nineteenth and early twentieth century Russia. Pogroms were actively encouraged by the Tsars' government.

Politburo
The Political Bureau of the Central Committee of the Communist Party of the Soviet Union. Its members make the major policy decisions and are therefore the most powerful men in the U.S.S.R. It was established in 1919, during the Civil War.

Presidium
(sometimes spelled Praesidium). The Politburo was renamed the Presidium during Stalin's last years, but after the downfall of Khrushchev in 1964 his successors reverted to the name Politburo.

Proletariat
In a loose sense it means the working class. For Marx and Engels it was a technical term meaning all those people who do not own any of the means of production. This could include people who in terms of their education, attitudes and habits would be loosely described as 'middle class'.

Proletarian Revolution
The point in history when, according to Marx's and Engels' theories, the proletariat seizes power from the bourgeoisie. After the Proletarian Revolution and an intermediate phase called the Dictatorship of the Proletariat (see above), Communism (see above) is achieved.

Redemption Payments
The system by which the peasants repaid the government for their land after the Emancipation of the Serfs in 1861. The payments were made in annual instalments, but many peasants were unable to keep up, and redemption payments were cancelled in 1905.

Repair Technical Stations
Government workshops set up in the 1950s to repair tractors, ownership of which Khrushchev had transferred from the machine tractor stations to the collective farms.

Republic
A system of government in which there is no monarch.

Romanov
The family name of Tsar Nicholas II and his ancestors.

Russification
The policy pursued by 19th century Tsars who aimed to wipe out nationalist sentiment by forcing all their subjects to learn Russian and by discouraging local culture and customs.

Satellite States
Countries whose foreign and economic policies are closely aligned with those of another, more powerful country. East Germany and Poland are two of Russia's satellite states in Eastern Europe.

SEATO
The South East Asia Treaty Organisation. An alliance (based on the ANZUS Pact of 1951) set up in 1954 to prevent the spread of Communism in South East Asia. The founder members were the U.S.A., Australia, New Zealand, Britain, France, Pakistan, the Philippines and Thailand. SEATO was dissolved in 1977.

Serf
A peasant in Russia prior to 1861 who was effectively the property of his owner, and absolutely subject to his owner's authority. The serfs were emancipated in 1861 by Tsar Alexander II.

Socialist Realism
A style and content in books, poetry and the visual arts favoured by Stalin and Zhdanov, who wanted the arts to reflect Communist progress, and to deal with the social and political lives of ordinary people.

Soviet
Literally means 'council'. The workers in Russia's cities elected soviets in 1905 and 1917, and these were developed into the local, regional and Supreme Soviets which govern the U.S.S.R. at present. The local Soviets are the equivalent of English borough and district councils, and the Supreme Soviet is the parliament of the U.S.S.R.

Sovkhoz
A State Farm in which the land and equipment is owned by the government and the workers are employed as wage-earners.

SOVNARKOM
The Council of People's Commissars, which was the cabinet of the U.S.S.R.

Sovnarkhozy
Regional Economic Councils established by Khrushchev in 1957 in a vain attempt to make economic planning and administration in the U.S.S.R. more efficient.

Stakhanovism
Willingness to produce more than the required work norm. Alexei Stakhanov, a coal miner who broke records in the 1930s, became a national hero and exemplar, and the Stakhanovite movement encouraged other workers to copy him.

Titoism
President Tito of Yugoslavia refused to obey the policies dictated by Stalin in the late 1940s, and Titoism was a term applied to any Communist government which deviated from the instructions that the government of the U.S.S.R. gave.

Truman Doctrine
In 1947 U.S. President Harry S. Truman announced his determination to assist any country threatened with a Communist takeover, and to prevent Russia from spreading her influence any further.

Tsar
Means 'emperor'. The title held by the rulers of Russia up to 1917. Formerly spelled Czar.

Tsarevich
Son of the Tsar – the title held by the Tsar's eldest son and heir.

Warsaw Pact
An alliance established by the Warsaw Treaty of 1955 by the U.S.S.R. and including all her satellite states.

Zemstvo
An elected district council. The Zemstvo system was set up by Tsar Alexander II in 1864 and gave the Russian Liberals a limited experience of politics and local government. The Zemstvos became a breeding ground of Liberalism.

Index

General Index

Page numbers in italic refer to illustrations, though in most cases there is also relevant textual material on the same page. 'G' in front of a page-number indicates a reference to the Glossary.